THE FINEST LINE

THE GLOBAL PURSUIT OF BIG-WAVE SURFING

THE FINEST LINE

THE GLOBAL PURSUIT OF BIG-WAVE SURFING

WRITTEN BY RUSTY LONG

FOREWORD BY TOM CARROLL   AFTERWORD BY GREG LONG

INSIGHT EDITIONS

San Rafael, California

CONTENTS

FOREWORD
BY TOM CARROLL

"**WHAT IS IT** that makes you want to ride waves like that?"

I imagine that all the humans plastered over the extraordinary pages of this book have been asked that question many times. It's a good question, and the answers would be as simple or complex as the various surfers' minds, themselves. While it can be a large ask for many just to sit by a raging sea and feel comfortable, there's one great truth for me: The turmoil of the ocean engages a reflective, mirroring effect in my soul.

The thrill of surfing began for me the first time I stood up on a board back in the late 1960s at seven years of age. Why was it that my first surfing buddy was suddenly nowhere to be found when the waves reached four-plus feet? Granted that was kinda big at our age. But he owned the only fiberglass "speed board" around, and where was he? I was lower down on the equipment ladder, with just a rounded-off polystyrene foam block. His board was left for the taking, and I just couldn't resist. Fear was right there in my skin, very clearly under my skin, tingling, shivering with adrenaline as I set forth down the beach into a strong current running out past the slamming closeouts just north of the Newport Surf Life Saving Club.

I had no idea what I was getting myself into. All I knew was that the waves looked like the images of Hawaii in the book I kept at my bedside, *A Pictorial History of Surfing.* I had fantasized about riding those waves, and it was that visual world that catapulted me into taking the necessary risks to prove myself at something I loved most.

This awestruck, freckly kid from Sydney imagined that Oahu's North Shore was the one and only place where the biggest waves were ridden on this planet, and it pretty much stayed that way for the next two decades. An introduction to the equipment used on these waves was my next wholehearted focus. Being naturally drawn to the curves and the idea of riding long narrow boards built for speed—the needle-like boards I pictured leaning against the imposing frame of Da Bull and under the arms of Gerry Lopez and Barry Kanaiaupuni—sent me into a stratosphere all my own.

This was way before we knew about buoy readings, and the lack of clear-cut information ignited our imaginations via the swell rumor mill churning out across the North Shore. This energy would turn with the wind and spread like wildfire; it was terrifying and intoxicating all at once. Just one look in the eyes of 1980's Waimea lone star Darrick Doerner, sporting the idea of a closeout swell arrival during our first week of three months on the North Shore, was enough to send us under a double-decker busload of internal drama . . . or was it a more subtle tipoff via the quietly disturbed, intense shift of Roger Erickson's eyes. Roger set the pace at Waimea from my angle; for him there were no such things as leashes. It was like one long swollen fishing story, our own brand of craziness forming human characters around a dream of being a Big-Wave Rider . . . without the added flotation devices and Jet Ski assist.

While the tide may be running out from this elder's viewpoint, a new tide is flooding in, flooding the younger charger's mind. Never before in surfing history has the mix been so potent. XXL Awards, Big Wave World Tours, ramped-up safety technologies, support crews, and the intrigue around a multitude of forecast charts at our fingertips and blaring in our faces via smartphones . . . all providing the cunning illusion that somehow *we know what's happening.*

What I know is that there's one common thread among us—a glint in the eye, a driving desire to be in the action.

As this book displays, the dream has spread worldwide. Surfers from all walks of life are now trying to answer the question, matching it with that look in their eyes, rising to the challenge. Rusty Long's unpretentious human eye, applied to the images and choice of text in this book, may help you move a little closer to why anyone might want to approach oceans the way we do.

INTRODUCTION

JUST AS THE WORLD has undergone accelerated progress in all manner of things, so too has the harrowing sport of big-wave surfing. Over the time period covered in this book, from just after the turn of the century until 2014, the sport has been taken to completely new levels where expansion, progress, and ever-increasing risk have occurred all over the world at a rapid pace, resulting in the most dynamic era in the history of the sport. Feats that were once very rare, like paddling into fifty-foot-plus waves, became normal. Waves considered unrideable or even unapproachable, like the giants at Teahupo'o and Shipsterns Bluff, became rife with chargers yearning to be towed into the craziest waves possible. And size barriers were redefined with the progression of tow-surfing at deep water venues.

Setting the stage for these advances was a worldwide passion for exploration that helped uncover more big waves in a remarkably condensed amount of time than ever before—from giants in populated European zones, to mutant slabs in remote Australian waters, to the obscure, deep wilderness of the Cortes Bank, one hundred miles out to sea. These explorations have been a defining element of this era and have led to some of the biggest waves ever surfed, at places still in their infancy as surf breaks, where we still don't know exactly what is possible. Another dimension in ocean power that people choose to interact with was opened, and there is no looking back.

It has been an incredibly fortuitous, exciting, and often nerve-wracking time to be a big-wave surfer. A perfect amalgam of elements came together to make possible advancements that have allowed this dedicated generation of surfers to explore, pioneer, and ride these enormous waves with such efficiency. To start, accurate swell and weather forecasting designed specifically for surfers became easily accessible on the Internet, hence available to and understood by most. The first step in riding giant waves is being there when the waves happen, which can be a rare occurrence, at times hard to predict, but that has gotten a lot easier. At the same time, communication methods multiplied, making sharing information about likely swell scenarios instantaneous, and with that more people showed up for the classic days. This created many landmark events with supersession phenomena, where charging was at all time highs, and the possibility of a historic ride was increased simply by having large numbers of people present pushing each other. During this time, travel also became easier and people with the cash to chase swells around the world at the drop of a hat did just that, turning chasing big waves into more of a year-round pursuit than it had ever been. After all, somewhere in the world is almost always pumping, and for many of the best surfers, it is hard to sit still knowing that.

The introduction of the Jet Ski into the surf scene was perhaps the biggest factor in assisting big-wave progression. The tow-in surfing boom around the millennium, most prevalent at Jaws and Maverick's, opened the door to the pioneering of many other waves. Places like the Cortes Bank, Nazaré, Belharra, Cow Bombie, and the big slabs, which were unapproachable via paddling, all came into play because of the Jet Ski, which still is the go-to tool for many of these extra-large, extra-heavy sessions.

The Jet Ski played another role as well: It was the catalyst to paddle into bigger and bigger waves and get back to the basic trinity of man, board, and wave. Tow surfing reached a state of disarray with excessive use and crowding because it was so easy for anyone. The best surfers in the world became fed up with how things had temporarily devolved. In a monumental shift, they collectively decided to leave Jet Skis behind unless the waves rendered them absolutely necessary. The quest to find out just what that absolutely crucial wave size is defined the later years of the era, where paddling into bigger and bigger waves was the core mission, resulting in the astounding

progression of paddle surfing and the biggest waves ever to get muscled into.

At the core of this progression is human desire. High risk yields high reward, and once you are accustomed to this elevated sensation of life it is hard to look back. It gets in the blood. It becomes a lifestyle, a devout discipline and ongoing quest for these brave souls who put themselves into this realm of one of Earth's most powerful and majestic forces, and tap into that energy. This is a finite group, a fringe society, and a deep brotherhood composed of solid, colorful individuals, all with an element of craze simmering somewhere inside that drives them to this pursuit.

These highly skilled big-wave masters deftly perform arguably the most difficult athletic art with a grace and necessary intuition that only comes from a lifetime of accumulated knowledge, developed only after spending much time in heavy ocean conditions. Prominent figures of the sport, like Shane Dorian, Mark Healey, Grant "Twiggy" Baker, Greg Long, Nathan Fletcher, Kohl Christensen, Dave Wassel, and Pete Mel, have led the charge into this peak in big-wave history.

While unwavering in their ability, those who choose this pursuit operate in an environment that can never be controlled. Big-wave surfers are constantly reminded how small they are when out of nowhere a rogue wave leaps up one hundred feet further out than normal and lands with dismembering magnitude, or when a wipeout breaks or dislocates something in the body, or when somebody dies. These are the realities those who choose this lifestyle face every time they paddle off the shore or jump off a boat when conditions are serious. The danger, excitement, and triumph create bonds that run deep. It breeds a family of international compatriots who work together and collectively advance this sport, incessantly searching for that finest line in the ocean and down the face of a wave, dancing on the fine line between risk and reward.

NORTH PACIFIC

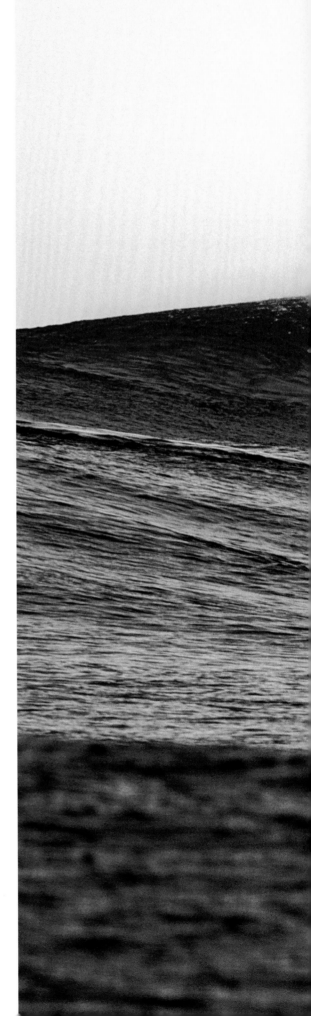

More big waves have been ridden in the North Pacific's diverse waters than anywhere in the world. With Hawaii and California as focal points, and mainland Mexico as backup, this ocean has spawned big-wave surfing's earliest roots and nurtured the greatest evolutions of this singular pursuit.

Big-wave surfing has gone global, but the epicenters of the sport remain the consistent, stalwart monsters of the North Pacific. These are the ultimate proving grounds—where palpable progress occurs, and where the greatest collective gatherings regularly take place. Devout big-wave surfers spend the vast majority of the Northern Hemisphere winter between California and Hawaii, their lives and travel dictated by each swell event. When the seasons shift, a short trip south to Puerto Escondido completes the North Pacific big-wave triangle.

With Maverick's, Cortes Bank, and Isla Todos Santos on Mainland North America, and Jaws, Waimea Bay, and Oahu's outer reefs in Hawaii, the North Pacific is globally unique in terms of quality and quantity. From October through March, the storms that produce the North Pacific's spectacular waves can develop at any time. Usually, they are spawned in the cold waters of Russia's Kamchatka Peninsula or Alaska's Aleutian Islands. From these brewing points, the swells are directed by the influence of jet streams—sometimes hitting Hawaii hardest, sometimes California. On particularly large swells, giant surf can hit Hawaii, continue across the Pacific, and light up the entire coastline from Oregon to Baja. Due to the vastness of the Pacific, large swell events often arrive with pristine conditions, unmarred by storm-associated weather, making the North Pacific the best place in the world for clean, consistent big waves. Year after year, the region's powerful waves draw the best big-wave surfers in the world. The biggest and best of these experiences, and the stories behind them, are revealed here.

RIGHT: Brad Gerlach fading on a pristine, mountainous peak at Cortes Bank.

MAVERICK'S

IN THE RUGGED WATERS of Northern California, just south of San Francisco and out beyond the ominous rocks off Half Moon Bay's Pillar Point, looms the notorious icon of California big-wave surfing: Maverick's. Since the 1990s, Maverick's (or Mav's) has been an epicenter of the sport—an imposing venue of pure triumph and tragedy. It is a daunting arena, often shrouded in harsh winter elements, and it attracts a hardcore cadre of surfers.

Spiking from the depths and unloading with debilitating force, the waves of Mav's are a rare phenomenon: awe-evoking and sometimes beautiful, but never friendly. Powerful North Pacific swells channel their way through a series of deep, underwater canyons that focus their raw energy into near-perfect A-frame peaks a quarter mile off the coast. It's an ideal bathymetric situation where the abrupt change of depth morphs swells into giant, tubing waves when they hit the underwater ledge.

For many, surfing Maverick's becomes a lifelong, sometimes fanatical pursuit. Dedicated crews have tested—and sometimes gone beyond—the limits of human capability here. Some of big-wave surfing's most heroic feats have occurred in this lineup—as have the tragic deaths of Mark Foo and Sion Milosky, two of the most qualified individuals in the sport's history to have passed while surfing big waves. Many others have endured near-death experiences, surviving impossible hold-downs and oxygen deprivation. The number of injuries the waves have dealt—all manner of dislocations, breaks, blown eardrums, concussions, and body trauma—is enormous. Most approach the lineup with utmost respect and in full awareness that Maverick's is an unforgiving environment where anything is possible.

Maverick's has seen several defining eras in its short history. Its modern story starts with Jeff Clark, whose legendary 1980s solo surfing exploits in the region still inspire awe and bewilderment. Later, through the '90s, a crew of Santa Cruz surfers (led by Richard Schmidt, Darryl "Flea" Virostko, Peter Mel, Zach Wormhoudt, and Ken "Skindog" Collins) charged with gusto, alongside a Bay Area crew led by Shawn Rhodes, Matt Ambrose, and Grant Washburn. Collectively, they put Mav's on the map, learning the wave as they went, swell by swell.

Peter Mel, with calculated, intense charging and superior surfing skills, is still of the best in the lineup nearly twenty-five years later.

OPPOSITE: Ken "Skindog" Collins, a hard charging fixture of the Mav's lineup for two decades, is just as passionate in his forties as he was in his twenties, nabbing this bomb in 2012. "I was licking my wounds from the beating I just took when all of a sudden a massive glassy lump appeared 100 yards outside of me," explains Skindog. "I was over from the crowd, and this wave came right to me. I did not want it, but Shane Dorian yelled loud and clear, 'Go Skinny.' So I decided I would pretend to paddle since you never back down when Shane calls you out. Next thing I knew I was at the top of this monster glassy wave, and my instincts kicked in, and I just pointed it straight down and went for it. I flew down the steepest and deepest drop of my life and felt like a cat clewing onto a tree."

TOP: Contest day, February 13, 2010. Mav's reached a summit of absolute glory where size and perfection were met by skill and desire, resulting in one of the most historic days in big-wave surfing ever.

RIGHT: The boat launch at Pillar Point Harbor.

"Surfing in the early '90s at Maverick's was an epic time," Mel says. "There was a group of guys on every swell, pushing the limits of what could be done in the Maverick's bowl. Guys like Richard Schmidt and Vince Collier showed us the way, and the rest was up to us with experimentation. I'm glad we made it through alive."

Maverick's, however, did claim one life during this era. Mark Foo, one of the most established big-wave surfers in the world, drowned after taking a wipeout in 1994. His death further woke everybody to the reality of the wave's power and treacherousness, thickening the air around Mav's.

Tow-in surfing came onto the scene in California in the late '90s, and another era developed with it. Many of the guys who were pushing the limits of paddling embraced Jet Skis, and for the next five or so years, most of the big days were "tow days." Amazing rides went down, and the wave was approached like never before.

With this tow-in boom, paddle-surfing progression at the break stagnated. But interestingly, almost as quickly as tow surfing was popularized at Mav's, so too did it fade away. This happened for various reasons. The number of tow surfers inflated fast, and teams were often composed of surfers who weren't capable of paddling the place—an increasingly common worldwide predicament that was questioned by both experienced tow surfers and paddle purists. Jet Skis were eventually outlawed in the Monterey Bay National Marine Sanctuary (which includes Mav's) by NOAA, who cited water pollution as the primary factor for the decision—a red

herring, but it worked. Unless the buoy readings were over twenty feet, when Jet Skis were still deemed legal, hard-nosed authorities enforced this new law, guaranteeing big-money consequences to violators. It curbed the tow surfing but also presented a problem for their use for water safety, an issue still at hand. Legal issues aside, many of the best surfers grew disenchanted with Jet Ski–assisted surfing, preferring the primal experience and challenge of solo individual against great force. They wanted to chase that feeling, unassisted by personal watercraft, and they wanted to go bigger.

The return to this simple pursuit ushered in the latest era at Mav's. Starting around 2006, a substantial amount of next-level paddle surfing started going down. Many of the old guard who pioneered the lineup were still out there, picking off gems with their veteran experience— alongside an ever-growing generation of young chargers from around the world.

Communication advances and ultra-accurate swell forecasting made swell chasing more prevalent than ever—and at Mav's, skilled and dedicated surfers, passionate rededication to paddle surfing, and a number of epic days produced historic sessions and high-risk progression. But then, sadly, tragedy struck again.

Hawaiian charger Sion Milosky passed away in March of 2011, during his third session at Maverick's. It was a big, wild, windy day, late in the season, and conditions weren't optimal. Milosky was surfing with his good friend and fellow goofy-foot surfer Nathan Fletcher, a Mav's veteran. By all accounts the two were surfing the place backside (backs to the wave) unlike any had seen before—taking off ultra deep on waves well into the forty-foot range and pulling off crazy rides.

About an hour before dark, Milosky caught a big wave, but was bulldozed at the bottom and most likely shoved into the deep currents that hold people down on the first part of the reef. He was under for at least two waves, and wasn't seen in the lineup again. Few people were still out, and nobody was doing dedicated water safety. Milosky went missing without much notice. By the time he was recovered at the harbor rocks, it was too late.

Milosky's death solidified the harsh reality of big-wave surfing once again: Even the strongest, most dedicated athletes could succumb to the power of the ocean. This stomach-turning reminder helped spur the movement for greater safety measures we see today. Milosky was a great, inspiring man—and despite his passing, Maverick's continues to compel others of his ilk.

OPPOSITE AND LEFT: Peter Mel has been leading the charge at Mav's since the mid 90s and is one of the most accomplished, highly skilled big-wave surfers of all time.

THESE PAGES: Nathan Fletcher
(above) and Derek Dunfee (opposite).
Concave management at Mav's.
Classic Thanksgiving swell, 2008.

ABOVE: When Shane Dorian brought his guru antics to Mav's in 2010, he lived up to expectations, surfing the place with utter brilliance and taking incredible lines on very critical waves, while always hunting for the biggest lumps possible. This wipeout occurred on one such lump. He was the only one who wanted that wave and it proved to have too much bump on the face to manage, sending Shane on the longest underwater journey of his life. The incident inspired him to develop the first inflation wetsuit, which has since redefined big-wave safety.

OPPOSITE: Dorian explains his fascination with Mav's: "When it's not putting the fear of God into me, Maverick's has its awesome moments."

MAV'S CONTEST 2010
THE DAY WE'D BEEN WAITING FOR

The El Niño winter was in full swing when the Mav's contest came around in February 2010. A constant stream of swells were freighting across the Pacific at lower-than-usual latitude. California and Hawaii had been hubs of nonstop activity, and the best surfers had spent the winter testing limits and feeding the momentum of the paddle renaissance. By the time the contest came around, people were on top of their game.

When the wave models took shape for the contest, speculation was all over the map as to whether Mav's was going to be approachable. An intense, tight-nucleus storm was approaching relatively close to the coast, tracking in as close as 1,000 miles, and producing forty-six-foot seas at its core. The swell's size and proximity to land almost guaranteed that Mav's would be in the fifty-foot zone—but borderline unruly, due to the proximity. The waves would be of a size and character people hadn't paddled much; in years prior, waves that size had dictated towing as the mode of operation.

The decision to hold these contests is often difficult. Local weather, as well as swell size and quality, are deliberated heavily (and sometimes contentiously) by a panel of surfers and contest directors. Once the "go" call is made and the wheels are in motion, there is no stopping the event. Fortunately, the final decision to run the 2010 event was decided democratically, via a vote by all the competitors. It was a new way of going about things—and a good one, because it allowed the competitors to turn their opinions into action and put the collective knowledge of the surfers to use.

Everybody suspected that massive surf was on tap as the votes were cast. Five of the competitors voted no because they thought the waves were going to be too big or raw, but nineteen competitors wanted to test the limits of paddle surfing at Mav's. The contest was on, and Half Moon Bay was set for a historical gathering of the best big-wave surfers in the world.

Most of the competitors were staying at the plush Oceano Hotel on Pillar Point Harbor. There, I met up with Grant "Twiggy" Baker. He was in pure relaxation mode—no apparent nerves for a guy who was going to go mad the next day. The weather outside the sliding door was bleak: gray and drizzly with a 15-mph south wind, just as it had been forecast. The talk of the town was on the possible conditions. Was the surf really going to be massive? Would the unfavorable weather linger?

Both the offshore Papa and California buoys were gone, beaten to uselessness by the winter's massive, persistent swells, so no real-time buoy data was available twenty-four hours out. But everyone had a gut feeling that something substantial was coming.

ABOVE: 2010 Mav's contest opening ceremony.

RIGHT: Alex Martins has a fervent passion for Mav's and has built his life around surfing the wave, relocating from Brazil to San Francisco. He's on the short list of guys always looking for the biggest bombs, evidenced by this ultra critical takeoff during the 2010 event.

The near-shore coastal buoys were twenty-two feet at seventeen seconds when we all awoke on February 13—a scary (though not surprising) buoy reading. I loaded onto the boat of legendary big-wave photographer Rob Brown at dawn, along with my brother Greg, Twiggy, Dave Wassel, and Mark Healey. We wanted to get out early and evaluate the lineup before the contest, and hopefully get in a quick surf.

The morning was very still, cloaked with a steely overcast hue and pounding with the thunder of waves. It's always an intense feeling creeping out of the harbor at Pillar Point. As soon as we rounded the jetty, we got our first sight of the mammoth swell lines and felt the power of the ocean. We knew it was going to be huge.

There was one person in the water when we pulled up. No one knew who it was, but we were surprised to see somebody out so early. We watched like hawks, and after ten minutes we saw the first real set looming. Massive swell lines stood up way outside; it was evident the set was going to mow over the guy in the lineup. The waves were going to break on the second reef, no question, where they do when they get above the fifty-foot mark—bad news for the lone surfer.

But they were going to be way bigger than fifty feet. This was the biggest set any of us had witnessed at Mav's, and this solitary surfer was sitting on the Bowl—the usual takeoff spot, where all the waves had broken since we'd pulled around the jetty, and where this set was going to smother. We looked at each other with disbelief: not only was this what was in store for us, but this lone surfer was about to get dealt a horrendous cleanup.

Then he did something astonishing. The first wave snuck past the second reef without breaking and loaded onto the Bowl, every bit of forty feet and thick, and the surfer, like an assassin, turned around and took an incredibly technical vertical drop.

"Who the hell was that?" we asked between cheers. "It's got to be Shane Dorian." But no one knew if Dorian was around or not; he wasn't in the contest, and he hadn't been spotted the day before when everyone had gathered for the event.

The next wave was around sixty feet—a dinosaur. It broke much farther out than where the anonymous charger had been sitting; it would have absolutely eaten him. "That guy is so lucky he rode that wave," we agreed. A couple more waves of similar size followed, showing us what the day had in store. The surf was huge, but it was also mysteriously perfect and looked approachable. We quickly geared up.

A couple minutes passed before we saw the surfer paddling back out. Sure enough, it was Shane Dorian. There was no one else it could have been—aside from a couple of the guys on our boat, or a few others who were making their way out on different boats for the contest. It was an amazing feat, with no room for error—paddling out into the unknown at dawn and riding a heroic wave to evade an enormous beating. It was his first session ever out there, his first wave. That was Dorian, operating as he does: completely next level, with Jedi senses and a deep desire to ride waves most wouldn't.

Healey and I scrambled into our wetsuits. Twiggy, Greg, and Wassel had heats coming up, and they didn't want to risk taking a beating before the contest started. Healey and I were alternates, though, so if we wanted to ride a wave that day, it was then. Dorian's wave was a major inspiration, and that set was critical in deciding where to sit. I didn't want to get caught

LEFT: The opening ceremony for the Mav's contest happens at the start of every winter. It is a time when big-wave surfers from around the world get reacquainted, pay respects to the venue and each other, and get pumped for another impending season at Mav's.

ABOVE: Brazil's big-wave kingpin, Carlos Burle.

ABOVE: The combination of exaggerated size and westerly angled swell allowed waves to get ridden from the outside second reef through the traditional "Bowl" takeoff section, creating the possibility for big tube rides, which rarely happens at Mav's. Rusty Long, pre-contest hour.

PAGES 34–35: Grant "Twiggy" Baker on his semifinal bomb. This amazing ride earned him 10 points (a perfect score) and later the prestigious Ride of the Year award at the annual Big Wave Awards. It was as technical, challenging, and risky as a ride gets.

by one of those things, so when I jumped off the boat I paddled outside to the second reef.

Sometimes you get gifts of waves in your surfing life. It seems to happen every couple years or so—maybe more, for the best of them. Five minutes into my surf, one of those gifts of a wave came right to me. The lineup was hard to determine out there on that outside part of the reef. I did my best to gauge it in comparison to

usual lineup markers, but also intuitively sat on a patch of boils roiling up from irregularities in the reef below—that felt like the spot.

Sure enough, the first wave of a big set came right to me. It looked perfect, and I was in the spot. I turned, got scooped into the wave, and glided down a big, ultra-smooth wall, feeling comfortable. Once I made my bottom turn I realized the channel was a long ways

"SOMETIMES YOU GET GIFTS OF WAVES IN YOUR SURFING LIFE."

twisted in every direction, but fortunately not in the train-wreck-violence type of way. Some wipeouts are just gentler than others, and this one, despite how it looked, was gentler. When I surfaced, the entire channel, which had steadily filled in with boats, was screaming and cheering. It was the peak moment of my surfing life—a wave of a lifetime.

I paddled back out and Dorian asked me what had happened because he'd heard the screams. I told him I'd gotten a tube. Soon as I said it, I could tell he wanted one. On the wave he rode a few minutes later, that's just what he got. Mav's was breaking unlike any of us had experienced before. The handful of us out there for that morning moment traded waves in what became a peak moment of our surfing lives. After forty-five minutes, the competitors for the first heat paddled into the lineup, chomping to surf, praising us all, and took the torch for a historic day of competition.

It was the biggest, best, most approachable Mav's anybody had seen, and the contest incentivized guys to really go for it. But it was a tough day to be in a competition. When the surf is that big, you don't want to work against the clock. It's hard to paddle out and just go. Many great surfers didn't catch the wave they hoped for because of this, but others found their rhythm in the forty-five-minute window they had—in arguably the biggest waves ever in a competition.

Twiggy was one such individual who shined; he rode two of the most incredible waves of the day. Being the tube-savvy surfer he is, he paddled out into his first heat with deliberate intent. On his first wave, he executed. The wave didn't give him the easy roll in. It was critical drop he knifed into and got off the bottom just in time to lock himself into an enormous barrel, and traveled as far as he could before the wave clamped and denied an exit. Still, the work was done. He got a near-perfect score while clearly showing his intentions for the day.

Twiggy went out for his next heat looking for another incredible wave, and halfway through lined up the ride of the day. He free-fell from the apex of a solid fifty-footer as it lurched forward into a massive hole in the ocean. The wave broke mere feet behind him at the bottom, and the avalanche of foam buried him. He looked toasted, but against all odds rode

out of the foam seconds later. It was a 10-point ride and later in the year won the prestigious Ride of the Year at the Billabong XXL Awards. But he didn't have a backup wave and failed to advance. That's competition, but also slightly unfitting for the guy who rode two of the best waves of the event.

So many noteworthy rides happened during the competition: Peter Mel's cutback on a bomb; Carlos Burle's multiple breathtakingly big waves; Chris Bertish's consistent charging. There were some terrible wipeouts, too. But Shawn Dollar of Santa Cruz, a noncompetitor, caught one of the standouts during the small break between the semi and the final. Without any hesitation, Dollar went out and muscled into the biggest wave of the day. It measured out at fifty-six feet, and still holds court as the biggest wave paddled into at Mav's. That wave propelled Dollar onto the main stage as a key player in the big-wave arena—a role he has remained committed to with constant success.

At the end of the day, South African Chris Bertish won the contest. He did so by surfing smart and charging hard, finding the waves he needed to advance through his first two heats. He grabbed two good waves in the final as conditions became more challenging and many of the finalists lost steam. He did all this while jet-lagged from the long flight over from South Africa, and with the highly spirited athletic determination he has tapped over many years of hard charging and endurance pursuits. He was a fitting winner: a people's champion.

Everybody who entered the water that day had a ride, a wipeout, or an experience that will stick with them forever. It was one of those rare days where the combination of waves and human desire conspire to create something spectacular and seldom replicated. It was unquestionably one of the best big-wave events in the history of the sport—a defining moment in the dynamic evolution of self-powered big-wave surfing.

Ken "Skindog" Collins, who's seen it all at Mav's, summed it up well, "The 2010 Maverick's surf contest was one of the greatest team efforts to push the level of big-wave riding in history. Having the world's greatest big-wave riders all together and having a clear chance to take on one of the biggest paddle days in history, with an organized attack and safety, allowed guys to have no hesitation in risking their lives to challenge these giant waves."

away, and what was in front of me looked like it was setting up to be a giant tube. I hadn't seen a situation look like that before. The scale was just so much bigger. Still, I knew the best option to potentially make the wave was to try the tube, so I set my line and angled for it—and sure enough, I ended up inside the biggest barrel of my life for a few completely surreal seconds. It had no exit. I got swallowed and thrown and

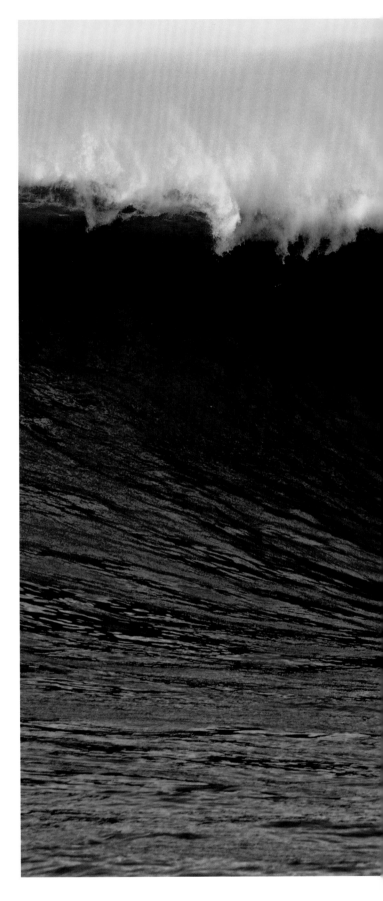

THESE PAGES: In the years preceding the 2010 event, Santa Cruz's Shawn Dollar had quietly begun muscling into some of the bigger waves on hallmark days. As an alternate in the 2010 event he had to watch from the sidelines as the biggest, best Mav's most have seen unloaded. When the 30-minute gap between the semifinals and finals temporarily opened the lineup to surfers, he pounced. "I was frothing all day. I wanted to surf so bad. I had dreamed of that day for years. It's still the best day I've surfed out there in the eight years I've been going out there. When the break came I was like a caged animal that was let go. I sat in a spot I felt was right, but I had no idea. It only took ten minutes for that set to come, and it was massive and had a ton of waves in it. It was the biggest set I've ever been in out there. I kept seeing one wave way back in the set stand way above the rest, and I waited for that one. When it finally came it was surreal. I had meditated on that wave, I had waited years for it, and now it was in front of me. I remember thinking, 'This is my shot I have to go!' I put my head down and paddled as hard as I could, and it lifted me up and put me in the wave."

ABOVE: Twiggy, finding the tube during his first heat of the morning.

OPPOSITE: A true Mav's veteran, Zach Wormhoudt on a bomb.

TWIGGY ON MAV'S

Twiggy Baker has unquestionably been the individual who has surfed Mav's the hardest and at the highest level over the past decade. His approach has been about calculated commitment on the biggest, thickest of waves that break on this reef—waves that often only he is looking at. He rarely makes a mistake or falls, and session-by-session adds to his collection of legendary rides, along with the occasional legendary wipeout. His prowess at Mav's has earned him two contest victories, both on years the waves were legitimately forty feet plus. His relationship with the wave is that of a savant—one of the few ever seen in the sport on waves at this level of consequence and challenge.

RL: Coming from South Africa, how did you commit yourself to surfing Mav's, and what were you hoping to accomplish out there when you set about doing it?

TOP: Twiggy, Maverick's.

OPPOSITE: Twiggy (left) and Darryl "Flea" Virostko (right), two of the best ever at Mav's.

TWIGGY: I didn't necessarily set out to accomplish anything. What happened to me with Maverick's was that I got there and my first day out there was a perfect day, and we had a couple perfect days over the next few weeks, and I just fell in love with the wave. Coming from Cape Town, with the messy, windy, raw big waves that we get there, perfect Maverick's was a completely different big-wave experience, and I just wanted to surf it and surf it and surf it. It became a passion. And then, after getting into the contest, I realized there was a possibility of getting paid to surf. That changed my perspective a bit. As soon as I got invited to the contest I knew that if I could win it, it would change my life. My priorities changed from that moment.

RL: Surfing the wave looked like it came very naturally to you. Was that the case?

TWIGGY: Initially it didn't, but I think because I spent so much time surfing out there the first two seasons it might have appeared like I caught on really quickly. But what in fact happened was that

Grant Washburn was in his manic "notch" phase, trying to beat everyone for the most sessions of the year, and I just tagged along. We surfed it so often that it might have appeared I became accustomed to it quicker than other people. It also suited my style of surfing. The perfection, compared to the chaos of Cape Town, made it feel like it was an easy wave to surf, and all my time in hollow waves over the years really helped. But that whole "notch" thing, and the amount we surfed it over the years, helped my performance level. Just surfing so much—south winds, north winds, small days—that's what really helped give me an edge out there. Ten thousand hours, right?

RL: What was your lifestyle like during those years when you were hanging around Mav's? How did it play into getting so on top of your game in this lineup?

TWIGGY: Ha—well, the lifestyle should have been detrimental to getting on top of our surfing game, but it was just a wild time. I ended up falling in with the San Francisco crew: Grant Washburn,

Randy Cone, Jeff Harrison, Ryan Seelbach, Lance Harriman. We would just surf all day, then drink all afternoon into the night for months at a time. A weird kind of drinking, too—not partying or anything like that, and never once did we go to nightclubs or anything, but after the surf we'd go straight for beers at the brewery and on days with no surf we'd drink at Tommy's Tequila Bar from 3:00 in the afternoon till 10:00 at night. Bizarre drinking patterns. That's what we were about and I don't know how that could have helped, but we were focused on the surfing—Ocean Beach and Maverick's. That was the lifestyle. Drinking and surfing and not being very healthy—no training, no kind of yoga, probably not even drinking enough water, but surfing Ocean Beach was almost enoug to pull it off. Times have definitely evolved.

RL: You won the 2006 contest in flawless conditions, not missing a beat the entire day. How were you feeling that day? Did you have that sense you were going to win?

TWIGGY: The honest answer is yes. It sounds arrogant, and there is arrogance in there, but it has more to do with confidence. But I did feel like that, that I was going to win, and the whole way through I kept catching waves that gave me more confidence, and it's just a feeling that you get, and I had the same feeling in 2014 when I won. So I've been trying to focus on getting that feeling for events, and one way to do it is just to really enjoy it. Enjoy being at a contest and competing. Enjoy surfing these types of waves with no one out. That's a big part of it. That's what I did that 2006 day. That confidence—it's a weird feeling, it's a really weird feeling. Almost as if you can do no wrong. It's like when you're playing pool, and you're on a run, and you just walk up to a shot, and you know you are going to get it. The difficulty is getting that every time, and I've been working on my mental conditioning to do that. Just focusing on getting that feeling of being light and enjoying myself. I just go out and focus on catching waves and stay positive, because I know it's a great day out there.

RL: How about your win in 2014?

TWIGGY: That contest was different. By the middle of the semifinals it was a mess; it wasn't really enjoyable anymore. That became a whole different mental game. In the final, people fall away. Anyone who's had a bad wipeout might not want to be there in the final—saw that with Anthony Tashnick in 2014. It's tough to keep wanting to catch really big waves. It's all about keeping that focus through the whole final, especially toward the end of the final, to keep wanting to catch the big waves. I think if you can make the final in these big-wave contests it's actually easier to win that heat if you can stay strong. It was a real mental game in 2014,

and I was lucky because I caught my waves early. Toward the end of that final, I didn't want to catch any more waves.

RL: What have been your most elevating experiences at Maverick's? Was your semifinal wave in the 2010 event the best ride ever for you out there?

TWIGGY: My first ever wave out there on the red Gary Linden board set my course. There's a whole story behind that wave. I'd just paddled out to have a look. All of the best guys were out and a fifteen-wave set—beautiful long period, eighteen-foot waves—came though, and I kept moving more and more toward the bowl and eventually the last wave of the set—the biggest one—came right to me. I had to go; everyone was shouting at me to go. I was hesitant, got caught up and airdropped out of the lip, reconnected and made it, went around the corner, then kicked out. Washburn, Jeff Clark, Peter Mel—everyone who was anyone was paddling back out and had seen it. I could have so easily wiped out on that takeoff, but I made it. It was such a fine line. If I had wiped out I would have probably broken that board or the leash, gone through the rocks, and that would have been it, gone home, tail between my legs. But I made it and got onto the alternate list the next year because of that, and it was the only year where there was a vote of the alternates and the winner got in the contest automatically, which I won.

RL: What a pivotal moment!

TWIGGY: It was such a fine line between being stuck in that lip and somehow making it. The parallel universes that splintered off from there gave my life a whole different direction. That one

wave, that one moment, that split second in time. So that's one of the waves. The other one is the 2010 semifinal wave. That whole contest is a bit of a blur. There was no planning or thinking about strategy, getting into a feeling—it was just pure fucking terror. No flotation back then, bad leashes, crazy. I can't really even remember the day, or that wave, really. Fear was just the overwhelming sense. But I do remember a moment of that wave—again, another split second. As I started paddling for it there was a little ramp at the top that forced my board onto the inside edge and it started to track to the right, which basically was going to take me over the falls, in the lip, while I was still lying on my board. I was saying, "Oh my god, oh my god," and then finally it corrected itself. That was a moment where things could have gone completely wrong. I also remember the moment after my bottom turn. I was looking for the barrel, because that's what we were doing all day, looking for the barrel on that second section, but I could see it was kind of crumbling and I wasn't going to make it, so I straightened in front of it. I remember the foam coming over me and thinking, "Okay, you're done, never going to survive this foamy," but the foam shot over me and didn't touch me inside, no pressure on me whatsoever, and I was like twenty feet deep inside it, no pressure at all, then boom, out the front, on a fifty-five-footer.

RL: What has been your scariest experience?

TWIGGY: Surfing in the fog. I've had two or three sessions in the fog and I still haven't learned. It's very scary in the fog; you can't see the lineups or when the waves are coming. I've been caught inside once in the fog and got pushed through the rocks. The fog scares me. Don't surf if it's foggy.

NELSCOTT REEF

NELSCOTT REEF IS LOCATED a half mile off the coast of central Lincoln City, Oregon. Despite its proximity to this busy coastal town, the wave broke for years with only a small audience of local surfers, remaining unknown to outsiders. Eventually, the local crew realized it might just be a legitimate setup and began exploring the lineup.

To help get some scope on the place, John Forse, a Lincoln City surfer, invited up a couple of qualified guys to give an outside opinion.

TOP AND ABOVE: The two access options to get out to the reef at Nelscott: beach launch or the river outlet.

OPPOSITE: The contest morning of 2010: Some of the biggest and best Nelscott ever seen and the first time a serious paddle day was to go down on the reef. Looking at the unruly ocean before the event, all bets were off as to what would unfold.

Accepting the invitation, Peter Mel and Adam Replogle, both at the forefront of California tow surfing at the time, decided to skip a Mav's swell and make the drive to Oregon in 2003, Jet Ski in tow. They'd seen a few photos of the place looking big, clean, and shapely—motivation enough to take the trek into the bitter cold and see what the wave was about.

After their first session, they were impressed. Lincoln City indeed had a legitimate wave. On what was a run-of-the-mill day down at Mav's, they towed into beautiful thirty- to forty-foot waves at Nelscott by themselves. Pictures of the session quickly circulated, and by the time they'd returned to Santa Cruz a new spot was on the greater big-wave radar. The local crew began riding the spot on a regular basis, and John Forse created an annual tow surfing contest, drawing many of the best teams in the world. There were good waves for a number of these early events, and Nelscott steadily gained status.

As the paddle-surfing renaissance progressed, the movement eventually spread to Nelscott. It started with short paddle-only expression sessions between the semis and final of the tow events in 2008 and 2009, and when the 2010 event was announced, it was billed as the first-ever paddle event at Nelscott. The short expression sessions had revealed that it was a great wave to paddle, and the surfers wanted to keep the momentum moving in that direction, so this was an exciting development. Then came the day nobody expected.

FIRST TIME'S A CHARM

An uneasy atmosphere permeated the cliffs overlooking Nelscott Reef on the oddly warm morning of November 2, 2010. The swell, as anticipated, was the biggest anybody had ever seen there. Speculation was rampant as the surfers gathered to watch distant peaks unload in the early light. "Is that even paddleable?" was the common murmur. Relentless thirty- to fifty-foot-plus waves reeled off both corners of the reef, raw and unruly with mist cloaking the air. A high tide added extra chunk and disarray. The ferocious-looking, disorganized sea appeared extra daunting from a half mile away, with all the tumultuous movement around the reef and huge reforms detonating on the beach break inside.

But the contest was on and a solid crew was there for it. Despite the nerves and uncertainty, everybody was ready. With a bit less tide and a bit more sun as the morning progressed, things began looking more inviting. Still, nobody knew what to expect. Nelscott had always been considered a tow spot because of its big playing field. Everything about paddling remained in question: lining up and actually catching a wave, getting caught inside, and the severity of the beatings. But the sun was getting higher, and an offshore wind was cleaning things up and dispersing the ominous early-morning mist. A classic day was coming together. I was in the first heat along with Shawn Dollar, Chris Bertish, and Carlos Burle. We were the guinea pigs.

Just getting to the lineup took more than an hour. It was an all-hands-on-deck affair getting the Jet Skis down the single, narrow boat ramp that dropped onto the beach; surges bounced off the cliffs, throwing around huge pieces of driftwood. Once the Jet Skis were in the water, the next task was getting past the twenty-foot, tubing beach break. For those without lots of Jet Ski experience in big conditions, this was a difficult challenge. It became obvious that the surfers had to step up and facilitate. It took their experience as Jet Ski operators just to get people out and back in, and little by little the task was accomplished and a rhythm for the day developed.

I teamed up with Hawaiian Jamie Sterling to get out to the lineup; we had an easy run because he's a skilled driver and accomplished surfer. We did our best to study the lineup in the twenty minutes before the heat started. It seemed to have gotten even better. The wave had a pronounced double-up that we hadn't been able to identify from shore and waves would break nearly on the same spot. We'd never seen that on a wave this size, but it looked approachable.

With a combination of nerves and excitement the first-heat crew entered the water and the contest commenced. Within minutes, a solid set approached. It was hard to tell where it was going to break, and we were all a bit spread out. As good fortune would have it, a beautiful big wave came right to me, let me in easily, then peeled at a flawless speed for the first real ride of the day. An epic day on the reef had begun.

Communicating after our heats and figuring out the nuances of the place, we discovered that Nelscott was letting us in somewhat easily on the double-up ledge. The crew got the reef dialed over the course of the day, and the event worked as an extra catalyst to keep the momentum accelerating.

Everybody charged during this historic event. Dave Wassel, Peter Mel, Carlos Burle, Chris Bertish, Kealii Mamala, Jamie Sterling, and Anthony Tashnick all had impressive performances. But Kohl Christensen was the in-form surfer, making use of both the lefts and rights, firing on all cylinders. In his first heat, he rode a particularly nasty left that few other humans would have considered—a near fifty-foot horseshoe he attested was one of the biggest of his life. He kept going all the way though the final and earned himself the title. This groundbreaking event was a special day for everybody, and a monumental moment in big-wave pioneering. The day's rare conditions—70 degrees, offshore winds, extra-large swell—unfolded in waves Nelscott may not see again for a long time.

RIGHT: Rusty Long on the first wave of the event. "All of us were nervous being in that first heat, but the lineup was much more organized than it looked from shore. It was actually perfect and much less daunting from the water."

LEFT AND ABOVE: While most surfers were looking for the rights, Kohl Christensen had another idea. This insane ride occurred during his first heat, and he kept momentum all day to capture the win at this historic event.

TOP AND PAGES 48–49: The North Shore's Jamie Sterling is a fixture on the international big-wave scene and is one of the most prepared surfers in the business. A third place finish in this event set the stage for him to become the 2010–2011 Big Wave World Champ.

CORTES BANK

ONE HUNDRED MILES west of San Diego looms a shallow point of the ocean long fabled by maritime voyagers as a perilous zone of rogue waves and treacherous currents. It is an eerie, lonely piece of oceanic wilderness— raw, remote, and teeming with oversized sea life. Since 2001, this unruly patch of ocean has become the venue for some of the most dynamic moments in big-wave surfing, where life and death are a mere situation apart.

Once the southernmost island of the Channel Islands chain before succumbing to erosion and sinking below the ocean surface roughly 10,000 years ago, Cortes Bank is a unique underwater seamount. Though it's only a viable surf spot about three days of any given year, when the elements come together and winter swells hit with enough intensity, this sleeping giant comes alive, and the southwest corner of the Bank transforms into a quarter-mile surfing expanse that produces some of the most unfathomably powerful waves in the world—a grand display of force and form, and one of the most radical, high-risk arenas in the world. Just getting to Cortes is a risky endeavor, let alone surfing the place. Crews have to be completely self-reliant and prepared for any situation. Boat and Jet Ski problems, rescues, injuries, drowning—all manner of catastrophe are on the table out there, one hundred miles out to sea. Your crew is your only safety net.

Since 2001, when Mike Parsons, Brad Gerlach, Peter Mel, and Ken "Skindog" Collins pioneered a day that revealed just what the bank was capable of, scoring majestic forty- to sixty-foot-plus waves, nearly every favorable opportunity to ride the place has been taken advantage of. Those opportunities are limited: harsh winds and disorganized seas are persistent plagues at Cortes. But on the special days, when the elements cooperate, the Bank transforms into a big-wave wonderland.

The next opportunity to ride Cortes presented itself in 2003, when warm weather, light winds, and solid swell collaborated for two days of perfection. Greg Long, Mike Parsons, Brad Gerlach, and I were the solitary revelers in flawless forty- to sixty-foot waves. These were pinnacle days of our surfing lives and concrete evidence of Cortes Bank's status as one of the best giant-wave spots in the world. Because this was only a moderate swell, a mere twelve feet on the outer water buoys, we knew the reef was capable of generating enormous waves— likely the biggest in the world, with the perfect confluence of swell and light wind conditions. That was the kind of day our small expeditionary crew wanted—especially Greg and Parsons, whose desire to ride the biggest wave the Bank could offer had become an obsession. Nearly five years passed without incident at the Bank; eyes were on it, but the conditions never presented themselves. Then, in 2008, it happened.

OPPOSITE: Mike Parsons, one hundred miles straight out from his San Clemente home on the wave of the day during the first Cortes mission of 2001. This trip opened a spectacular new dimension in the big-wave world.

TOP: Photographer Rob Brown's boat heading out of Dana Point harbor at dawn for an early Cortes mission.

GOING ALL IN

A series of two back-to-back storms developed close to the Southern California coast in January 2008, churning up some giant seas. More than anything, they looked like rugged weather events—bringing what surfers call "victory at sea" conditions—but Greg and Parsons saw a six-hour window between the storms and had a gut feeling that Cortes Bank could be massive and doable. The first storm was going to pass by in the night, leaving a half-day window before the next was forecast to hit. In this short timeframe they saw potential for the winds to slack off. That plus the twenty-foot swell that was running meant there was a possibility to surf the biggest waves ever attempted at the Bank.

Still, it looked questionable. Residual rain and wind remained a strong possibility, and the swell could be largely disorganized. Greg and Parsons monitored it until the last minute, organizing everything as they watched, and assembled the team they needed, which consisted of veteran Cortes boat captain Rob Brown and surfers Twiggy and Brad Gerlach.

Surfline founder Sean Collins, the most prominent surf forecaster in the world, was crunching the weather and swell data for the crew, and his firm answer to Greg, Parsons, Gerlach, Twiggy, and Brown was "No. Don't go." It would be a terrible ride out with 20-mph south winds, and in Collins's opinion the ocean likely wouldn't clean up during the window between storms. They would have to contend with weather and big seas—all in a boat with very little shelter from the elements—conditions that would make for difficult Coast Guard assistance if things went bad. The risk was too high, the chance for success too low.

But Greg and Parsons were determined and in perhaps the most maniacal stage of their big-wave careers. They believed there was going to be a "window" and convinced the others they needed to go for it. Brown was the most reluctant. It was his boat, he knew it would be the most radical mission he had ever done, and he trusted Collins's advice. But big-wave surfers in pursuit can be a difficult breed to reason with, their determination infectious, and the crew set off from Dana Point on a eerie, stormy south-wind morning better suited for sleeping in than for a surf excursion to a deadly, skulking seamount a hundred miles out in the Pacific.

BELOW: Brad Gerlach at a defining moment and making the correct decision to pull out of the wave. A challenge of tow surfing Cortes is chasing the shifting peaks over such a big playing field and oftentimes not knowing if you're too deep or not deep enough.

RIGHT AND OPPOSITE BOTTOM: All involved in the Cortes mission between the storms snagged what still hold court as some of—if not the—biggest waves ever ridden. Greg Long (right), Twiggy (opposite bottom).

PAGES 54–55: Mike Parsons on the largest wave photographed during the mission. It measured seventy-seven feet and was the culmination of Mike's years of dedication to surfing the Bank. A bigger wave has yet to be ridden out there.

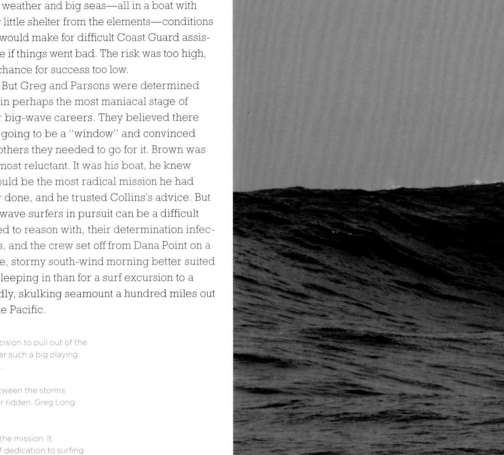

GREG LONG, TWIGGY, AND MIKE PARSONS ON CORTES

RL: As the preparation for this mission unfolded, it looked like a risky endeavor. Sean Collins was advising you not to go, and his forecasting opinion had usually been held in the highest regard. How were you feeling about making the final decision to go out there? What swayed you to pull the trigger?

GREG LONG: To be honest, there really wasn't any preparation leading up to this particular swell. From the moment that it showed up on the models, it appeared to be a complete write-off, with raging south wind and rain stretching from Oregon to southern Baja. It wasn't until about 2:00 p.m., the day prior, that the models suddenly changed and there appeared to be a small six-hour window of light wind out at Cortes. I immediately called Snips [Mike Parsons], who had seen the same change in the wind prediction as well. We then called Rob Brown, to see if he would be willing to take his boat out, and then Sean Collins and Mark Sponsler for a more detailed surf and wind prediction. Both acknowledged the same six-hour break in the wind. The problem was, the window we were looking to surf was in between two massive storms: the first a cutoff low that would slam Southern California with torrential rain and gale-force southerly wind,

and the second, the intense storm that actually created the swell we were going to ride. Every time we had surfed Cortes prior to this we would leave the harbor the evening before and take a slow overnight cruise—but doing it that way this time would have been a certain disaster given the conditions, so Snips and I began scheming. The southerly gale was supposed to subside around 9:00 a.m. the following morning, and the swell wasn't meant to hit Cortes until noon, so we figured if we put one Jet Ski on the back of Rob's boat and drove the other one behind it, we could make what is normally a ten-hour overnight cruise into a four-hour daytime sprint. The idea was downright crazy, and Sean, coming from a maritime background, tried to be the voice of reason. We were going a hundred miles out to sea, in hopes of finding a gap of wind in between two massive, unstable low-pressure systems. . . . But, if everything went according to plan and the forecasts were correct, it was doable and we would have the opportunity to ride potentially the biggest waves of our lives. That possibility was enough for me to ignore the elements, take the chance, and go out there. It all happened so suddenly I never had the time to get nervous or really contemplate my actions. The only preparation I made other than the

basic tow-surfing essentials was the purchase of a few extra EPIRBs [emergency position-indicating radio beacons] for the crew. I put mine in a dry bag and stuffed it inside of my wetsuit.

TOP: The Cortes washing machine. Disappearing out there this day was a very real possibility.

ABOVE: Brad Gerlach gearing up.

OPPOSITE: Twiggy, Parsons, and Greg Long upon arrival at the Bank.

MIKE PARSONS: I was super nervous. There was only a small window in between storms, and we just kept debating and waiting and seeing what was going to happen. That's what made it so sketchy—being right in between storms, not knowing if we were even going to get a window. Anxiety was pretty high. I remember the buoys being the biggest I'd ever seen at the closer ones like Point Conception, when we woke up at five in the morning the day of to see what the wind was doing. It had definitely laid down from the evening before, so we were like, "Shit, let's go for it." We just thought we might get a few hours to even see it—thinking it was worth going just to see if it was rideable and get a feel for how big it really was because we knew it was a special day in terms of size. To us it was worth the risk to just motor out there, and if it wasn't rideable or it blew out or it rained too hard, we could always just come back and not surf. But in the back of my mind, I figured we would ride it.

TWIGGY: If I'm completely honest about that session, I was in the dark. I had no clue what I was getting myself into. I was just listening to Greg, and I was his partner; Cortes was his wave. So basically, whatever he was doing, I was going to do it. I don't think I weighed in much on the decision; I just told him that if he wanted to go I'd back him up. I do remember sitting at Maverick's the night before while we were still deciding, and it was pissing rain, just a complete mess. And I remember thinking, "Shit, it's going to take a lot to clean that swell up before it gets down the coast." But when Greg called it, there was nothing else I could do. They called it on. And I guess if you're not gonna trust Greg Long and Mike Parsons on Cortes, then who?

RL: I understand the boat ride out was rough. Were there any second thoughts once you got into the open ocean?

GREG LONG: It was still raining and blowing hard south wind when we got to the harbor in the morning. The ocean was in a total state of disarray, with an eight- to ten-foot south wind chop crossing up a small northwest groundswell, but we weren't going to be deterred. We loaded one Jet Ski on Rob's boat, and I jumped on the other, taking the first shift driving it behind the boat. The plan was to ride the ski in twenty-five-mile shifts. If we averaged twenty-five miles per hour, we could make it to Cortes in four hours. Before leaving the dock we had one brief conversation where we all acknowledged the risk of what we were about to attempt, and that we would only continue forward as long we felt safe with the conditions. The moment things started to get sketchy, we agreed, we would give up and turn around for home. The second I came around the Dana Point Harbor breakwall on the ski, and began plowing head-on into the giant wind swell, I vividly remember

thinking, "There is no possible way we are going to pull this off." After the most abusive hour of my life driving a ski, I signaled for the boat to stop. Conditions had been so bad, we had only made it ten miles. We cruised for a moment in a slow idle, contemplating the idea of aborting the mission, when we all realized that the wind had just completely died off . . . right on time, as per the forecast predictions. Morale was quickly restored, and we decided to go for it. Little by little, the ocean calmed, and we were able to pick up speed and make up lost time. When we came off the lee of San Clemente Island, it was nearly glassy; the sun started to break through the clouds, and we began seeing the first long-period groundswells At that moment my

focus shifted—from worrying about whether or not we were going to make it, to thinking about the giant waves we were mere hours away from trying to surf.

MIKE PARSONS: It was a challenging morning. One of the engines wasn't firing right off the bat on Rob's boat, and it took some time before we got the motor going. And it was pretty eerie out. There was south wind and it was foggy—just an eerie vibe. I was definitely scared just thinking about how big it was going to be and what type of day it'd be like. As we motored out we were going too slow at first, and we were almost thinking we were going to run out of time. But once we got out a ways, things started to calm down a bit, and our spirits lifted. The wind wasn't too bad, and it actually almost got sunny about three-quarters of the way out. We were making good time, and things became more optimistic—like, "We might get a window here. This could be the day of our lives." I was definitely thinking I could ride the biggest waves of my life, knowing what the buoys were.

TWIGGY: I thought, "We're probably going to get out there and it's going to be a mess and we're not going to surf." That was my thinking. I picked up that Greg and Mike were nervous . . . but for myself, I was thinking the whole time that we weren't going to surf, and I was just going along there to appease Greg. That was kind of my mindset. Gerlach, on the other hand—he was sick as a dog with seasickness. And of course you know that we all had to drive a ski. One ski had to be driven behind the boat the whole way. Actually, when I got on the ski behind the boat, I thought, "What the fuck are we doing?" But I rode the last bit, and I was on the ski when the Bank came into view.

RL: What was the situation out there upon arrival?

GREG LONG: When we finally pulled up, it was so big—there were waves breaking in places I had never seen before. It was Twiggy's first time to Cortes, so we sat back and watched for a moment as I explained the dynamics of the lineup. We were conspiring a game plan as to how we were going to approach our session when Mike motored out the back and towed Brad into his first wave. I will never forget watching Brad let go of the rope and start chattering down the face of this massive swell. There was still a little residual south wind bump cutting across the lineup, but it wasn't until I saw Brad on the wave that I realized those "bumps" were a lot bigger than they looked. They were so big that they made our normal "west bowl" takeoff unsurfable. Brad fought to keep up with the wave, but it proved to be too fast and bumpy, and he was thrown from his board and thankfully drifted out the back before it actually broke. It was at that moment that the reality of what we were getting ready to do really sank in.

MIKE PARSONS: At a distance we were blown away by how much whitewater there was. We stayed way off the reef and unloaded the skis before heading over to the lineup. Immediately I knew the waves were the biggest I'd ever seen. It was reeling so far down the reef and the whitewater was so big from so far away. I'd never seen it like that—just full-on, constant waves. No breaks, no lulls. I got really excited. But when we got out closer to the lineup, I got worried again. I'd never seen so much refraction going toward the bowl. The swells were moving so fast and Brad and I were telling each other, "Whoa, this is the real deal! We can't make a mistake today."

TWIGGY: Well, we didn't have to wait for it to get good. We got there and it was fucking pumping. It was on. It did get better and better and better through the day, but when we got there, really you could tell straightaway it was surfable. But then again, we were probably oblivious to how big it was. We saw that the playing field of the white-water was miles and miles squared. It was hard to gauge the size of the waves; we knew it was big, but we didn't understand how big it was. So we just did what we had to do. Refilled the ski, which was difficult; got the other one off the boat, which was a fucking nightmare—getting suited up and ready to go probably took an hour, and in that time we were just normal, excited to get out there.

RL: How did your session start out, and how did it progress?

GREG LONG: As much as we would have liked to, easing our way into the session was impossible. Every set was massive, and trying to find and ride smaller inside waves was going to potentially put us in an even more dangerous situation. We went up the reef to the "north peak," where it was biggest and free from the south bump. From there, we waited for the biggest sets.

MIKE PARSONS: I felt really confident and excited, although it was pretty nerve-wracking. First wave I remember, I was freaked out because it was so bumpy. But once I made that first wave, I felt all the nerves go away and my mindset shifted. "Okay, give me the biggest wave," I thought. That's what we were there for. My board felt good—all my equipment did. I was definitely in a time in my life where I wanted it. I had that confident, comfortable feeling of "Let's get the biggest wave we've ever caught." I felt excitement more than fear at that point. The adrenaline started flowing, and I started thinking, "Get the ride of your life right now."

I remember Greg had an amazing wave, and he came back out and he was so stoked. We were screaming and yelling across the lineup. We weren't thinking, "Oh, we're going to drown today," or anything like that; we were just thinking, "It's on. Let's ride huge waves." While we were out there, things really started to progress. We rode quite a few for how big it was. I don't know how many each, but a lot. It was nonstop—five, maybe ten minutes between sets. It was the four of us,

so you could really pick and choose the gems and wait for the second waves in a set that were a little smoother—all that kind of stuff.

TWIGGY: A cringe moment came right away. Everything could have gone wrong. I drove Greg first. We didn't realize it, but there was a steady current running into the impact zone. So as soon as we stopped the ski, we were hundreds of yards up the point. I didn't realize that until it was too late, and then we saw a set out the back. We'd lost where we should be surfing, which was way inside of us, within five minutes. And we see a set farther out, and I just go, "Fuck. Okay, a set!" We went out to the top peak and then chased it in, and then I'm thinking, "This is too far away. Not sure where we are." I get Greg onto this thing, which at the top peak was eighty feet, easy. But he didn't let go, stayed on, didn't want it. As we kind of came off that wave, I see another set, outside but wide, and we had to race out to get around that set from where we were. If he had let go on that wave, that ten-wave set was going to close out to where he was. I never would have found him. He would have been gone into the square miles of foam. After, we went to the side; we talked about it; we stayed wide and just came towards the wave. Then it kept getting more and more perfect, and the tide got better. And the waves just kept getting better and better. Perfect, top to bottom. Perfect, perfect, clean waves, as big as you can imagine waves can be.

RL: Was it on your mind just how heavy of a mission this was as you were putting each other into the biggest waves of your lives?

GREG LONG: Before entering the lineup, Twig and I both acknowledged that this was going to be the biggest and most dangerous session of our lives. The lineup spanned almost a mile and the inside was a tumultuous cauldron of white wash and foam, with currents raging in all directions. If somebody fell on the north peak, or lost the ski during a pickup, chances are they would have been lost at sea forever. With stakes so high, and no backup safety of any sort, we simply acknowledged that neither one of us could make a mistake.

MIKE PARSONS: Yeah, we felt like we were in the zone. It was definitely on my mind the whole time, and we kept reminding ourselves that as much fun as we were having, we needed to stay alert and not make a mistake. At first I was riding waves pretty conservatively, making sure I positioned myself where I was going to make it. As the day went on and things got better, I started going a little deeper and edging up the reef. Cortes, it's a lot heavier if you surf it from the top of the reef than the end.

At the same time, I was thinking about my life. My wife was pregnant. I thought, "You know, if you drown today, you won't see your kid be born." I was totally aware that I could drown that day. I think I usually am when waves are that big. The few times I've surfed waves that big, I know that one mistake and I could drown. So that was on my mind—but more on my mind was, "I want to get the biggest wave I've caught." I was way more scared thinking about it on the way out than when I was surfing.

TWIGGY: Yeah, but we were just engulfed in the moment. It was afterwards, years, like when I talk about it now, that I just realize how lucky we were, how stupid we were. And the little bit of flotation we had, those little vests? Things are just gonna get ripped off you immediately. No leash. Gone. Fuck. Crazy, crazy, crazy, crazy. Greg was on a mission, though—the tall Cortes mission. He's still on it. He's emotionally attached to Cortes, like I am to Dungeons [in Cape Town]. You've got to watch that emotional attachment. It's dangerous.

RL: The best feeling during many big-wave missions is when they are over. How was that feeling after the session, knowing you had successfully ridden some of the biggest waves ever?

GREG LONG: I can honestly say that never in my life have I been so excited to see the sunset and be forced to leave the lineup on a big day as I was that evening at Cortes. As we began motoring away from the Bank, the wind started raging out of the south, and the next front stormed in, bringing torrential rain once again. As we were leaving, the

swell was peaking on the Tanner Bank buoy only a few miles away with readings of twenty-four feet at nineteen seconds—huge. Even though the surfing was over, navigating home in such conditions was still extremely dangerous. It wasn't until we were in the lee of San Clemente Island and conditions calmed down a little that we exhaled and began to celebrate. We all knew that we had just ridden the biggest waves and pulled off the heaviest mission of our lives.

MIKE PARSONS: The feeling was insane. It was dark, and we were all fine, with a huge sense of relief and achievement. That feeling like, "Wow, we just did something really, really special." For Greg and me especially, because people, like Sean Collins, told us not to do it. Nobody else was there; nobody even thought of it. Part of the fun of scoring huge waves is pulling it off with just your friends. It's becoming harder and harder to do nowadays, so when you do that, the feeling is incredible. It was amazing, 2008, and we surfed the biggest Cortes ever, alone. Those are the best moments. Cracking a beer, laughing, telling stories. The kind of stuff you live for.

TWIGGY: It was incredible. But there was some disappointment, too, because many photographs didn't come out. We risked death and obviously we were pumped, but then when we got back and we saw the photographs, we were kind of disappointed because some of the biggest waves weren't there. Rob wanted us to come surf the inside, but it was the eighty-foot peak out the back we were on, and we wouldn't come around into his view from the boat until the wave was almost over. It was really weird. And the film guy was seasick, and he missed the whole session, vomiting down below. We all knew that we rode bigger waves than Mike's wave, which won the XXL award that year, but that was the best photo. So it was a strange feeling. When you're breaking barriers, you want it to be documented.

RL: In hindsight, just how risky was the mission?

GREG LONG: We all knew the potential worst-case scenarios prior to going out that day. Never once did I feel that trip was "safe" or "smart." Looking back now, and having nearly drowned out there in much smaller conditions, I regard it as being probably the stupidest thing I have ever done in my life. At that point in time, my goal was to ride the biggest waves in the world. I saw an opportunity to do just that, and took a chance. I'm glad I did because it turned out to be one of the most memorable experiences of my life. I have still yet to ride, or see, waves bigger than I did that day and I don't know if I ever will in my lifetime.

MIKE PARSONS: Off the charts. One to ten, it was a twenty on the risk and stupidity scale. But then again, we'd done it our whole lives and we weren't new at it. At the same time, with the amount of support we had—and looking at what's happened out on that reef since that day—you just realize, "Whoa, we were completely out of our minds." We didn't have a medical team out there, or water patrol; we were just looking after each other, and it could have gone real bad. But shit, what are you going to do, right? It was one of those moments where you just say, "Fuck it, this is why we surf." It's not the smartest thing, but when you look back at it, you're sure glad you did it. That day was it. That's what I live for. That was the pinnacle of my surfing life.

TWIGGY: It was insanity. It's sessions and moments like that that make me really question if that whole parallel universe concept is real. So many things could have gone wrong that day, but they didn't— we just willed them not to.

OPPOSITE: Greg Long at home in San Clemente prepping for the Cortes mission. Missions to the Bank always require meticulous preparation, which Greg excels at.

TOP: Twiggy on a black diamond slope.

THE VOYAGE INTO PADDLING CORTES

As the push to explore the boundaries of paddle surfing grew, Cortes Bank became an inevitable target. Jon Walla and Evan Slater had bravely attempted to paddle the place during the first mission in 2001, but they were quickly cleaned up without riding a wave. Eight years later, big-wave surfing had progressed, and the idea was brewing for another attempt; once again, Greg was the driving force.

The El Niño winter of 2009 and 2010 was serving up plenty of swell, so turning the idea of a pure paddle mission into reality was a matter of finding a day with tranquil wind conditions. Veteran big-wave photographer Jason Murray had something up his sleeve: a connection through a friend to a 110-foot super yacht named Mr. Terrible, which was docked in the Newport Harbor, sitting idle. Being a savvy go-getter, Murray threw the idea out to the captain to go out to Cortes if conditions aligned. The captain and crew obliged, excited to do something different.

On Christmas 2009, the idea came to fruition. A swell was brewing and destined to arrive on December 27. It looked medium-sized, with a long interval, and it was set to coincide with a day of immaculate weather. All the ducks were in line with the boat, so we

got on the phone and assembled a first-class crew of talent. On the afternoon of December 26, Greg, Twiggy, Peter Mel, Mark Healey, Nathan Fletcher, Ramon Navarro, Alfy Cater, Kelly Slater, and I loaded up Mr. Terrible with boards, Jet Skis, safety equipment, and a few bottles of tequila.

It was a smooth cruise through a tranquil ocean that night, and we woke up just off Cortes Bank, refreshed and ready to surf. The swell was just starting to fill in, so there was no rush. We all ate breakfast, unloaded the Jet Skis (which would be used for safety), and hit the lineup. By midmorning, consistent twenty- to thirty-foot waves were breaking in serenely calm conditions up and down the reef. We had all gotten in the water by this time, and an easygoing session was taking place in beautiful midsized waves, with the occasional bigger set to keep us on our toes. In a perfect world it would have been slightly bigger, but for an experimental session it was sufficient. We surfed all day in clean, approachable, semibig waves. As we sat around the kitchen on the way home, drinking beers and passing around the tequila bottle, we concluded that we wanted to paddle Cortes at a substantially bigger size.

THESE PAGES: The first paddle session was amidst flawless conditions and a friendly swell. It was the ideal situation to test the waters in the traditional method. Rusty Long (above) and Ramon Navarro (right) exploring the wave's paddle potential.

TOP: Kelly Slater and Peter Mel evaluating the many board options on the first paddle mission. The crew was equipped for anything.

ABOVE: Nathan Fletcher eyeing the expansive lineup. With no markers to line up with or past paddle sessions to reference, this was very much a trip to the unknown.

On December 17, 2012, Greg started going into hyperdrive: another swell was brewing for a Cortes paddle mission. It wasn't a slam-dunk forecast, though. Winds were expected to be less than ideal, with predictions of 10 to 15 mph onshore. But the wave size was going be in the right range: not enormous like the 2008 between-storm tow-in mission, but much bigger than the 2009 paddle session. "Consistent forty-to fifty-foot faces" was Greg's prediction after analyzing the data, with some bigger waves likely at the top of the reef.

Greg had a plan, as he usually did. He wanted to include only a small crew consisting of Twiggy, Shane Dorian, Ian Walsh, and himself—an even number, in case it turned into a tow-in affair. But towing was unlikely. They were set on testing the fringes of self-powered big-wave surfing. They organized six Jet Skis that would do water patrol, to ensure maximum safety. Greg's motive was to catch the biggest paddle-in wave of his life, and he went about setting up all the precautionary measures for the small crew to do it as safely as possible. Safety awareness and equipment had come a long way since that day between the storms four years earlier.

He lined up Mr. Terrible again and began piecing things together in relative silence,

keeping his plans within the circle that was part of the mission. In this age of rapid communication, if you want to surf a session in relative solitude this is how you have to do it—otherwise you may end up with twenty or more people in the lineup, even one hundred miles out to sea, and crowds increase the danger of the situation. But despite Greg's attempts at keeping his plans quiet, word trickled out.

I wanted to get out there as well, but only Billabong personnel were allowed on Mr. Terrible this time. I was in communication with Peter Mel and Mark Healey, and they wanted a piece of it, too, so we began organizing. Mel was running the Quiksilver big-wave program at the time and was able to hire Rob Brown for the mission. Legendary Australian waterman Jamie Mitchell jumped on board as well, and at the last minute Shawn Dollar came down from Santa Cruz and rounded out our crew. We had two skis; our plan was to always have two people doing water safety within our crew, and take turns surfing. It wasn't quite the backup Greg had, but it was a safety net.

Word kept trickling out, and two other boats full of competent surfers were organized. One group was led by Garrett McNamara, who came out prepared with solid water safety, and another was a mixed crew who came out without even a Jet Ski for safety support, which was crazy. By the time the boats were being loaded up, Greg's clandestine mission had evolved into a crowded session.

The sea surface was oily smooth for the first fifty miles out to San Clemente Island, and for a moment we thought we might luck out with the winds. But when we rounded the island, the sea got much rougher. San Clemente Island is a dividing line; once past it, you enter true open ocean waters. The power engulfs you. And then, it's fifty miles to Cortes Bank. We powered on against a 15-mph headwind. These were not ideal surfing conditions—or boating conditions, for that matter—and after a couple hours of battering, we pulled up next to the solemn buoy on the edge of the lineup, its incessant bell tolling to warn of the phantom reef below.

The swell was just filling in, and the wind was on it. Aesthetically it was gross. The lineup looked uninviting, with mediocre surf at best— but conditions aside, there were going to be some big waves. By 2:00 it was getting large, and Greg was the first to go out. He was full steam ahead, and within minutes he'd stroked into a very bumpy, unruly forty-foot-plus wave. It was a wild ride from the time he stood up, bump after bump after bump, and two-thirds of the way down one of them finally thrust him

off his board. He deployed his inflatable vest to lessen the time underwater and surfaced before the next wave, a bit beaten up but okay.

There was a limited amount of time left in the day to surf, so nearly all the surfers there got into the lineup. Within our crew, Dollar and I volunteered to do the first shift of water safety. I wasn't feeling good about the conditions. It was inconsistent, windy, and now crowded—but the waves were getting bigger and bigger. Twiggy was the first to nail a good successful ride on a big one. Most other attempts, the guys couldn't keep up with the wave. That far out to sea, the swells move much faster than near-shore breaks, and the difficulty of keeping up on a big-wave board was evident. The challenges—and limits—of paddling large Cortes Bank were revealing themselves.

Most everybody was clumped together at one spot—the most consistent zone, but the occasional bigger wave was unloading farther up the reef. Dollar had analyzed the lineup longer than any of the other surfers, doing water safety for the session's first hour. While on the Jet Ski, he'd taken note of the larger waves fifty yards deeper in the lineup. He'd had a history of looking for megabombs after his Mav's wave in 2010. It was with that mentality, he jumped in the water and paddled past the crew to where those bigger waves were breaking, and where the danger factor increased exponentially.

BELOW: A clean Cortes wall goes off unridden. This was one of the first proper sets of the day and enough to get everyone buzzing.

I was his Jet Ski safety, and it worried the hell out of me seeing him that deep on the reef; if he went down at the start of a wave, I wouldn't be able to get him until he had been dragged way inside. After a frightening first attempt on a wave that knocked him off when he stood up and almost sucked him over the falls, he lined up his wave. It was one of the biggest that came through, and there was nothing pretty about the wave or easy about the ride. It was lumpy and wind-riddled, but he finessed his way over multiple bumps and troughs and down a streaking wall for a couple hundred yards, finally reaching the safety of the channel. All of sixty-plus feet, it was the wave of a lifetime—instant history.

The next set was the first of the day to boast multiple good waves. Twiggy, Healey, Greg, and Dorian were all sitting together, the deepest of the pack. Healey whipped it on the first one and screamed down a big face, but was gobbled just after he reached the bottom. Once again, the wave was just going too fast. I was doing rescue for him, too, so I started tracking him from the time he went down, watching the turbulent aftermath of the wave and keeping an eye on the one behind it.

Greg was on the spot for the next wave. He got to his feet and picked a good line down the face. In a circumstance that came back to the crowd factor, he ended up with another surfer on the wave. Garrett McNamara, who was using a motorized surfboard, came into the wave from farther on the shoulder. Boards like his were a new invention, unsuitable for controlled surfing because of their excessive weight and poor design, but he was testing it out that day. Seemingly, McNamara was not in control, and he veered into the line Greg was drawing—something he most likely wouldn't have done

on normal equipment, because he is a highly skilled, experienced big-wave surfer. But it appeared he was battling the board, and at the critical moment when Greg needed to make a bottom turn, McNamara was on top of him, forcing him to straighten out in a bad spot. Both guys were bulldozed, and the greatest struggle of Greg's life began.

An abandoned Jet Ski caught my eye alerting me that something was wrong. It was at least fifty yards farther outside than where Healey and McNamara had surfaced. I zoomed out toward it and quickly realized Greg's safety team members were all clustered in the same place. Something wasn't right. I pulled right up to them and, in the most sinking, terrifying moment of my life, saw my brother's unconscious body on the back of a sled, stiff and purple, getting straddled by Maui surfer and water safety specialist DK Walsh, who had abandoned his ski to dive in the water and grab hold of Greg's unconscious body, making a perfect rescue.

Greg, who was in peak physical condition and had trained both mentally and physically for such a situation, had been underwater for four waves. His flotation suit had malfunctioned and failed to inflate despite multiple efforts. The ocean bottom is very uneven out there, which can produce underwater eddy currents and cause water to pull in all directions with incredible strength. Greg had gotten swept around in these currents, and without the flotation to help bring him up he'd been completely at their mercy. Still, he'd persisted and persisted, and right as he neared the surface he blacked out.

LEFT: Mark Healey on the wave of the set before Greg's incident.

ABOVE: Rusty Long (left), Jamie Mitchell (middle), and Mark Healey (right) aboard Rob Brown's boat.

He recounted the whole experience in detail for *Surfing* magazine about a year later, after much reflection:

The hold-down of the first wave was so long and brutal that I contemplated staying down, knowing there was a good chance I wouldn't get to the surface for a breath before the next wave in the set rolled over. I decided to swim for the surface anyway. This was a pivotal decision that took what would have likely been a "standard" two-wave hold-down to

one that nearly ended my life. As I struggled for the top, I was mere feet away from the surface when I received the full impact of the next wave. Any remaining breath was forced from my lungs and my body was shaken into a state of shock. I immediately found myself back in the abyss, but now with zero oxygen in my lungs. My body convulsed radically, desperately begging me to inhale, but I was still deep, and made the very conscious decision that no matter what, I wouldn't. "I am fine; I am going to make it to the surface,"

were the only thoughts I chose to know. I allowed my body to relax and my desire to breathe momentarily diminished, allowing me to stay conscious long enough to hear the next wave of the set roll over my head.

. . . I desperately needed to get to the surface and breathe. The turbulence of the third wave was impossible to swim against so I climbed my leash, hand over fist. Inch by inch I fought my way up, eventually reaching the tail section of my board, which was submerged ten feet below the

surface. Cramping, numbness, and full-body convulsions returned. Any oxygen reserves remaining in my brain were exhausted and I couldn't get a solid grasp onto my board, so I let it go, taking one last desperate stroke for the surface. It was at this point that I lost consciousness.

THESE PAGES: The wave that nearly took Greg's life (above), the rescue (top right), and the Coast Guard extraction (right).

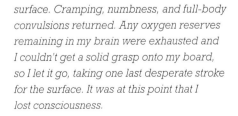

Fortunately Greg got close enough to the surface that once that final wave passed, the safety crew was able to grab him quickly. In addition to Walsh, Jon Walla, a firefighter and paramedic and Greg's longtime mentor and friend, was there on another ski, along with Frank Quirarte, another safety specialist, and the three of them got Greg on the sled.

By the time he was secure, Greg had been unconscious for just over a minute. We knew he was within the timeframe of a likely recovery if CPR was administered immediately. Walla yelled, "Gotta get to the boat for CPR," and we blasted over there as fast as we could.

It took about a minute to get to the solid platform of the boat, and in that time, as he bounced on the ski with the cold wind hitting his face and DK yelling his name, Greg's senses were alerted and his body knew it didn't need to be shut down any longer. As we loaded him onto the back of the boat he began to regain consciousness, and his body began the violent repairing process. His lungs hacked up foam, water, and blood; he breathed in and out and his body convulsed. CPR was never needed.

For the next three hours we monitored him, keeping oxygen flowing, periodically rolling him on his side to get fluids out. He slowly regained orientation and awareness, but he wasn't in the clear yet. "Secondary drowning" was a real concern, and he needed to get to a hospital. We called the Coast Guard—the one

lifeline out there—and requested an extraction. But despite their support, this event confirmed what we already knew: you needed to be completely accountable for yourself at Cortes Bank. They were on another call. It took them three hours to arrive.

Upon arrival, the Coast Guard helicopter lowered a rescuer with a basket, a technical feat considering the big swells and the rolling of the boat. Greg was secured in the basket and brought to the bow. Murray, Quirarte, and the Coast Guard jumper held him down as the chopper came in tight for the pickup—a delicate precision operation. The basket was strapped to the line that was dropped, and once the all-clear was given, Greg was ratcheted up. The jumper grabbed another line, strapped in, and was hoisted up. Within a minute, they were out of sight and the scene was suddenly, eerily quiet.

The stark reality of the risks of these missions to Cortes kicked us all in the gut. We were all very thankful that everybody had done their part to save Greg, and that the safety measures he'd set up had ended up saving his own life. But the question lingering in everybody's mind—Greg's more than anybody's—was "Was that worth it?" After this blunt lesson of absolute accountability, and without Greg as a driving force, nobody knew if there would be another surf mission to the Bank.

A little over a year after this incident, Greg wanted to go back out to Cortes. He'd had an emotional year of contemplation, but ultimately decided he wasn't going to give up his passion. He'd continued surfing big waves, but now he did so with a slightly slower approach and an increased level of fear.

OPPOSITE: Shawn Dollar did water safety for the first hour of this session and noticed some of the biggest waves were coming in up the reef past where the crew was clumped together. When he paddled out, getting one of those waves was his goal. "The swell was building, and it was getting more consistent out at this top peak. No one was sitting there. I paddled there so I could sit alone and focus on catching a wave and not jockey with the rest of the guys. Being out there was full commitment. The swell was building and the biggest waves I've ever seen were starting to come in. No matter how far out I sat it wasn't enough. I finally paddled so far out that I thought I was going to be way outside of the next set. When that wave came I thought it was going to break on my head. I paddled as hard as I could hoping to get over it, and as I paddled up it I had an impulse to spin, and I did. Next thing I knew I was bouncing down the face and bottom turning. I linked into a few more sections and literally felt like I was surfing for my life. When I was safe in the channel I was so thankful and filled with emotion. It was the most amazing moment of my life. I was so lucky to have made it. I was done after that. I felt like I had walked away with my life. I didn't need to push my luck anymore." This ride set a paddle world record at sixty-one feet.

"After my accident, my confidence was absolutely shattered," he explained. "I felt in a way that going back out there and facing my fears, I might be able to find a little bit again."

So when Greg saw a day that looked ideal to paddle into some smaller-scale waves with pristine conditions, he pounced. Once again, he set up a solid safety net and organized to go out with just Twiggy and a film crew from a documentary series he was working on.

The day to surf the Bank was the day after the 2014 Maverick's contest was called on, and Twiggy told Greg that if he won, he wasn't going to fly down directly after the contest and boat out all night for the mission. As fate had it, Twiggy won, and Greg was on his own.

He entered the water and surfed pristine twenty- to twenty-five-foot waves by himself for seven hours, rebuilding his confidence and starting a fresh relationship with the Cortes Bank—his special place in the surfing universe.

"I knew that going back out to surf the wave that nearly took my life would undoubtedly be the greatest mental challenge I would ever experience in my surfing life," Greg said. "I was right. I was nearly sick with fear when I pulled up to the Bank that morning. Embracing and moving through that fear was one of the most difficult things I have ever done, and consequently I experienced one of the most rewarding sessions of my life. It was comforting for me to experience the Bank in an entirely different light than I had previously. In the end. I did walk away from that session with a little more confidence—but more importantly, the experience of a lifetime." The relationship continues. The Bank beckons.

LEFT: The conditions for Greg's solo surf at the Bank after his non-fatal drowning were pristine.

ABOVE: Greg on his return mission in January 2014 to make amends with the Bank.

BELOW: There is always a sense of overwhelming relief on the trip home from Cortes Bank.

ISLA TODOS SANTOS

TOP AND ABOVE: En-route to Isla Todos Santos by road and sea.

OPPOSITE: The sun was nearly setting, and Brad Gerlach thought he and Parsons were done for the day. They were in the channel actually starting to pack tow gear back into the Ski when way out the back a really big lump appeared. Within a minute Gerlach was on this sixty-eight footer that won him the XXL Biggest Wave award that season. Then he really was done for the day.

TWELVE MILES OFF northern Baja's bustling port town of Ensenada lies the desolate Isla Todos Santos. This island's world-class big-wave break, Killers—a boil-riddled right-hand reef off the northwest tip of the island—has been the hunting and developing ground for Southern California big-wave surfers since the 1980s. Throughout the '80s and into the '90s, Todos was the mainland's answer to Hawaii, and the principal big wave in the region. Its cobalt-blue, glassy big waves filled the pages of magazines, and a talented generation of surfers (led by Mike Parsons and Evan Slater) became accomplished big-wave riders with Todos as their training ground.

When Mav's came onto the scene in the early '90s, expanding California's big-wave scene, Todos took a back seat. But even though attention went up north, Todos still demanded the spotlight every few winters with a giant day. One such day occurred in February 1998, right in the guts of a raging El Niño winter, when Taylor Knox caught a fifty-two-footer that earned him the first-ever $50,000 prize purse for the biggest wave caught in a season. It was a huge accolade and a reminder that Todos could produce some of the tallest waves on the West Coast.

The tradition of Todos breeding Southern California big-wave surfers has continued. Greg and I were privy to this. Growing up in San Clemente, we were around guys like Mike Parsons and the McNulty brothers, standouts at Todos. We looked up to them, and their stories about the break were epic.

Greg developed an obsessive passion for Todos, postering an entire wall in his bedroom, right above his bed, with nothing but images of Killers. We drove there religiously to surf days big and small, and by the time Greg was in his late teens it was apparent he was going to have a prominent future riding big waves. He had an unwavering dedication, as well as the requisite desire, skills, and guts, and over the following years Todos was integral in grooming him into the champion surfer he became.

Killers has bared its teeth in many memorable extra-large sessions. But one historic swell shines above the rest—and a dedicated group decided to use their bare hands to approach it during the peak of the tow-surfing boom.

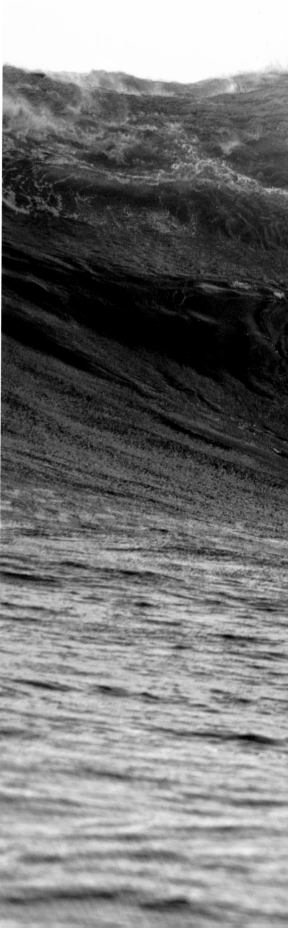

LEFT: Rusty Long

TOP: Jamie Mitchell and the kind of Todos that makes for big smiles: blue, glassy, and big.

ABOVE AND OPPOSITE TOP: Gary Linden (above left), Jon Walla (above right) and Mike Parsons (opposite top) have collectively ridden a lot of big waves at Todos. Linden is one of the oldest aficionados, still out on the big days anywhere in the world, inspiring the younger generation.

TODOS AT ITS BIGGEST

It was December 2005. I was in Hawaii, hanging with Greg and the Hawaiian crew, when a storm headed back home and demanded our attention. It was projected to track abnormally low off the Southern California coast and send direct west swell to Todos. This was looking to be the biggest the spot had seen in a long time. So, much as we wanted to stay in Hawaii, we headed back to the cold with Jamie Sterling, Mark Healey, and the animated South African charger Andrew Marr.

Word got around, as it does, that Todos was going to be massive, and a group amassed at Ensenada's main harbor at dawn, ready to jump on the local panga boats. But it wasn't business as usual. The panga drivers weren't hustling the way they typically did. Usually surfers could show up, link up with a boat driver, throw their gear on board, and sit back for a forty-minute ride out to the island—enough time for some last-minute breath-holding exercises and mental prep. Today, though, the harbor was moving at snail's pace. The drivers weren't even around first thing—highly unusual.

It took a couple minutes to track down somebody who knew what was going on. The swell forecast had been all over the news, and maritime warnings had been issued prohibiting boating activity. The harbor was effectively closed off: no boats could leave, and the authorities were not budging. The local boat drivers had been told they'd lose their captain's licenses if they went out. So it looked like a no-go. Everybody was at a loss, stuck in the harbor listening to the seals bark and watching giant plumes of white wash surge over the jetty as the morning ticked on.

We were trying to make it happen any way we could, appealing to every captain in the harbor to see if they could get an exception. Finally, we had a breakthrough. Alejandro Berger, a filmmaker from Uruguay and an old friend, was with us for the mission. His good vibes and South American way of handling business got him a meeting with the harbormaster. He went in and spoke frankly, telling the official we were all professionals and were there because the surf was massive and the boat drivers were ready to drive us out. The drivers weren't worried about the high-sea situation, Berger explained, and we needed to get out to the island for this opportunity of a lifetime. It took some convincing, but the harbormaster finally relented. We just needed to sign our lives away. A basic document was created stating that any mishap was off their hands. We signed, passed word to the large group of others in the same situation, and were off, albeit a couple hours late.

Greg and Healey had managed to sneak out of the harbor at Hotel Coral on Jet Skis with photographer Jason Murray, so they'd arrived on time. The boat ramp had been chained off, but they'd gotten under it with inches to spare while getting yelled at. When we neared the lineup, Greg was already streaking down a bomb, well over forty feet, nearly on his own in the water. Andrew Marr, Jamie Sterling, and I got on it, along with an unfortunate south wind that sent a nasty bump up the face of the waves. Late we were. But it was massive, and getting bigger.

The lineup began filling up with the other crews. Consistent forty- to fifty-foot-plus waves unloaded. The south wind threw massive bumps up the face of the waves, making things difficult and dangerous. The occasional wave was getting ridden, but it was very high risk.

Most called it quits—the probability of making a wave was too low for such high consequences—and only about ten people were left in the water when the biggest lumps of the day stacked up. Sterling and I were sitting farther out than anyone, at that point. I'd spent enough time in that lineup to know that if this set was any bigger than what we'd already seen, it would break farther out on the reef and clean everybody up. This happens all the time at Todos: waves hit the next increment of size, and break on a different part of the reef. Anybody who has surfed out there consistently has a cleanup story or ten.

The scale we were presented with here was bigger than usual, though, so Sterling and I began paddling even farther out, not wanting to take any chances. I glanced back: the other guys were stroking farther out, too, but slowly.

Then, the set was upon us—and when Sterling and I got over the first wave, we were shocked. The second wave was enormous, and despite our efforts we still were in a questionable place. We called out behind us, hoping to give the other guys a few seconds' notice, and kept sprinting out. It's hard to say how big the wave was in the moment—it was by far the biggest we'd encountered while paddling. (It later measured out in the seventy-five-foot range.)

In these situations, one's paddle strength is pushed to untapped levels. Only at the last second did I realize we were going to make it; we were up, up, up, and barely over. Everybody else was gone. My last sight as I looked back into the trough was of Healey and Billy Watson, an Aussie lifeguard on his first session out

ABOVE: A cleanup set for the ages, December 2005. For a sense of scale, those are ten-foot boards. This session can be seen as a turning point when the best surfers present reverted to paddle surfing on the biggest of days. One year prior this would have been a tow session.

there, in the absolute worst spot I had ever seen anybody. It was sickening.

Healey later explained that the blast of the lip somehow blew him into the air for several seconds, where he floated, weightless, before getting consumed. It was an unusual blessing for him—getting lifted by the shock of the explosion and pushed away from the initial, violent impact. Watson wasn't so lucky. He wore every ounce of the wave. He was a very fit individual and physically capable, but he looked like a ghost afterward—the look you see when people think they're going to drown. The wave was a session ender for most. Sterling , Andrew

Marr (who was in the channel paddling back out when the wave broke), and I were the three people left out in the lineup.

Fifty-footers kept rolling back inside of our location, but we refused to drift in. It was an uncomfortable situation—but after about an hour, we began moving in, and a few others paddled back out, Healey included. He'd had to fetch his board off the rocks by swimming to the treacherous shoreline. Being the rare specimen of surfer he is, Healey was still hungry for a big one. Most people get annihilated and are done—but Healey comes back hungrier. He ended up nabbing a couple over

the course of our session, which lasted through late afternoon.

This was a "survival of the elements" session and a turning-point moment in the latter-day progression of paddle surfing. A year earlier, this would have been a tow session; people were on the sidelines with Jet Skis the entire day, waiting to tow but not ready to paddle. Instead, they watched a few self-powered takers recalibrate the system at Todos. It was an inspiring session for those who did surf, reigniting the self-powered pursuit of the biggest waves the world has to offer.

PUERTO ESCONDIDO

THE SANDBLASTING GLADIATOR PIT of Playa Zicatela is one of the few places where truly large-scale, ultra-hollow tubes can be approached without the aid of a Jet Ski. Since the mid-1970s, when Puerto Escondido was slammed onto the rapidly expanding international surf map, this rare breed of beach break has received a constant stream of tube-savvy individuals looking to hunt down liquid caverns at the vibrant, Wild West–style surf outpost.

Like Pipeline, Teahupo'o, Maverick's, and Jaws, Puerto Escondido is a place people have dedicated their surfing lives to. Its one-of-a-kind essence resonates with particular surfers, hooking the psyche with a buffet of ultra-consistent, sand-bottom barrels. Many Puerto veterans are enchanted by one particular tube and chase that feeling again and again, always thinking the next swell might be the one. Sometimes the big tubes are elusive; sometimes they come easy. Regardless, seasons pass by, the tube count goes up, and the hunt continues.

When the beach gets above twenty-five feet and reaches its prime form, Puerto aficionados shine. The regularly occurring

Mack-truck tubes—coupled with the laid-back, nonconformist, sometimes-edgy, monetarily reasonable, quality lifestyle this stretch of coastal Mexico can offer—conspire to make this a special place in the surfing world. The local surfers are very proud, love where they live, and spend countless hours clocking tube time, with Coco Nogales leading the charge as the de facto mayor of the beach.

Puerto has seen its share of thirty-foot-plus days over the last forty years, and on big days, most in the lineup feel a special affinity for the place. That passion has aided in the progression and celebration of the paddle-in tradition here.

As much as anywhere, the risks are in bed with the rewards. Countless injuries and a few deaths—most recently, the passing of beach veteran and celebrated underground charger Noel Robinson—are the concrete evidence. The waves carry a shattering amount of power. The submarine canyons that feed directly into the northern part of the bay draw and shape the swell, carrying the speed and intensity of deep-sea energy. Nowhere else in the world does swell travel for more than three thousand miles and still reach heights of fifty feet, as it does at Puerto when giant South Pacific swells reach the coast. The way the swells magnify and spike from the canyons into apex peaks is a magnificent spectacle of nature, and the platform for mind-blowing tube riding.

TOP: The harbor at Puerto is always calm, yet so close to the break—a testament to the dramatic underwater canyons.

ABOVE: The "Mexpipe" peak.

RIGHT: Ian Walsh on a proper canyon dweller.

It's hard to imagine a geographical situation more ideal than Puerto Escondido's. In addition to the submarine canyons that shape the waves, the Sierra de Miahuatlán mountain range, jutting east of the beach, benefits conditions. The warm ocean temperatures suck the air from the cool, pine-laden mountains nearly every morning; these offshore winds groom the lineup until about 10:00 a.m. This fairly predictable cycle makes it easy to get into a solid surfing routine and really tune in. When it's big, those serious about the wave are up before dawn and on it at first light to maximize their surf time before the wind switches. The more time in the water, the better, because it can be hard to track down the wave you want amongst the shifting peaks and erratic rips. On big days, catching three waves over the course of a morning is a successful session. Just getting one good ride is a success. That's the credo the best surfers approach the place with. Just find the one and make it count. Don't mess with marginal.

The challenges of surfing Puerto begin with getting to the lineup and end with getting to shore. The ubiquitous rip currents are your best friends getting out to the takeoff zone, but your worst enemy getting in. They are the constant element at Puerto. Time it right and a rip can pull you to the lineup in seconds—often the only way to get out when it's big. Lose your board and get stuck in one after a ride, or get caught inside on a paddle out, and a high-endurance challenge and

radical flogging may ensue. Everybody who has put any time in the lineup has stories of getting recycled into the impact zone by way of a rip and pushed to the point of exhaustion.

Puerto has traditionally been ridden without leashes—to minimize broken boards and avoid getting hit by your board during a wipeout—which keeps a level of accountability and order in the lineup. It is one of the only big-wave arenas where this is the case, and on big days a high-endurance swim is a given without a leash, which keeps a level of accountablility and order in the lineup. This no-leash tradition, which stemmed from the early chargers, isn't totally adhered to anymore, but was by 90 percent of those who surfed the place until 2010, when the tragic death of Noel Robinson rocked the Puerto surfing community.

An ultra-positive Puerto stalwart, Robinson passed away after a heavy wipeout. He was knocked unconscious and, leashless, there was nothing to indicate where his body might be. Had he been attached to his board the chances of his recovery would have been greatly improved. Instead, an hour of scouring the lineup passed before he was recovered—and by then, it was too late. From that point forward, many who surf the beach on big days use a leash. Every passing in the big-wave community brings blunt lessons. As sad as they are, the community responds to them, which has resulted in increased lifesaving prevention and protocol.

ABOVE AND RIGHT: Coco Nogales is the mayor of Puerto Escondido surfing and the best big-wave surfer to come from Mexico. Big Puerto is where his surfing thrives, and he loves it.

OPPOSITE LEFT: Raul "Rata" Haro, a Mexico City native with a past life as a big mountain snowboarder, has transitioned into loving the liquid mountains of Puerto.

OPPOSITE RIGHT: Oscar Moncada, one of Puerto's best, born and bred.

THESE PAGES: Noel Robinson had an intimate relationship with Puerto Escondido. He loved all aspects of being in Puerto, from the waves to the quality, simple life. He truly was one of those special people that was a pleasure to be around, whether you were a long-time friend or brief acquaintance. A bubbling source of positive energy, Noel was a treasured friend to so many people, spanning the many continents he traveled.

He had his life centered around surfing good waves and living simply, and didn't need much to fund his "priceless" lifestyle. He lived and worked the winters in California then dipped out to the warmth of Puerto come April. It was an ultimate cycle.

He was one of the best surfers to ride the beach and had more experience, intuitive wave knowledge, and style out there than just about anybody. He was always the first up in the dark making coffee, watching as the first hints of light revealed what kind of day it was going to be before choosing his board accordingly and getting out there before anybody—usually onto the wave that would make everybody else scramble to the lineup. Over his fifteen-plus years surfing the beach he rode countless incredible waves and played a multi-dimensional role as a legendary figure on the beach. Noel passed away when he was knocked unconscious on May 7th, 2010, during his final session in perfect ten- to fifteen-foot Puerto—a session he had been ruling all morning, doing exactly what he loved most.

WHEN GREG FOUND HIS RHYTHM

On July 26, 2009, Greg locked his relationship down with Puerto. He'd always found decent waves in the years before, but in this session, he synched with some of the best Puerto waves ever witnessed. The 2009 swell had real girth. Long, tapered, thirty- to forty-foot-plus walls bounced between the Far Bar peaks (at the southern surf zone of Playa Zicatela) and drained off with cartoonish perfection. Greg couldn't have had a better day to zone in.

His rhythm came in the later half of the morning, commencing when he stuck an airdrop on a forty-footer. This was followed by back-to-back caves—all within about thirty minutes. It was the first time he'd really applied his approach and understanding of big-wave surfing—gleaned from sessions around the world—to the beach. Finally, he had the Puerto riddle figured out.

I was about fifty yards away from Greg when he rushed the first bomb he airdropped on. I was in position to go on the left, off the other side of the peak. I'd just gotten back out from dealing with a caught-inside and broken-board incident and gave the wave a look, but wasn't feeling up to the backside challenge. I'd only been in the lineup again about two minutes, and I wanted a big right—not an enormous, sketchy left. I'd seen where Greg was on the peak, and when I turned back and looked in that direction, just after the wave passed, he was gone. I was blown away. I remember saying to myself, "Holy shit—he went!" As the wave exploded into the sky, I hoped for the best. It was the biggest wave I'd ever seen anyone take on at Puerto. The wave tapered down the line for about a hundred yards—still nothing. Suddenly, he flew out the back, glided as far as he could on the pullout, then started paddling back out like a maniac, making it out right before another set—another serious feat. That sequence set the tone. Each year since, he's done something very similar, tracking down some of the best extra-large tubes in every significant swell, developing a historic relationship with big Puerto.

RIGHT: Greg Long immersed in one of his many dreamy waves from the July 26, 2009 session.

"HIS RHYTHM CAME IN THE LATER HALF OF THE MORNING, COMMENCING WHEN HE STUCK AN AIRDROP ON A FORTY-FOOTER."

LEFT: Greg Long is always ready to go big in either direction. Since the July 2009 session, Greg has exercised extreme patience on all big days and come away with a mind-blowing ride nearly every time. The one-wave quota. Making it count.

ABOVE: Greg Long from the July 26, 2009 session.

A HOT LAP

It was June 2010, prime time in the season, and a big swell was in the water. Healey, Greg, and Twiggy paddled out from the harbor at first light without checking conditions. I opted to wait, scope the lineup, and see what we were dealing with before choosing a board to ride. As light increased, the guys made their slow paddle into the zone, and the morning revealed itself. The swell had a predominant southwest angle and seemed to be focusing at the Far Bar. It looked thirty to forty feet solid, with all the immense force a swell this size carries.

To be cautious, Healey, Greg, and Twiggy gave the main surf zone a wide berth. They appeared to be clear of any danger when a different-looking set began rolling in—bigger than anything the early light had revealed. All of a sudden they went from paddling in the open ocean to a possible cleanup situation. They began scrambling out and barely got over the first wave, only to find the next one bigger. They paddled like mad, Healey trailing behind ever so slightly. Twig and Greg paddled up, up, up, and got over, but Healey wasn't so lucky. He had

no option but to dive through the giant wave face, which was easy enough—but his leash popped, leaving him swimming in the depths.

He seemed to have two options. Swim back to the harbor, by far the safest idea, which would take a good forty-five minutes—or swim in, which was sketchy given the rips and the size of the swell, but which could potentially take only five minutes. But he actually had a third option. Somehow, he'd had a premonition that morning to stick a hundred pesos in the pocket of his trunks. He'd actually envisioned this situation—losing his board and getting stuck out the back—and had an idea.

He started swimming out, at a quick pace. Over by the harbor, fishing boats were making their morning departure, and Healey hustled to get in their line of sight. As one got near, he waved his hands and yelled, catching their attention, and the guys came by, wondering what the hell the gringo was doing. Healey jumped on and asked for a ride back to the harbor. They weren't too inclined at first, but then he dug into his trunks and pulled out the hundred pesos and the mood changed. He got to the harbor, ran back to where his board was on the beach, got back out there, and then nabbed the wave of the day.

ABOVE: Panga boat heading out from Puerto Escondido.

RIGHT: There is nothing better than getting spit out of a big tube, and Puerto is one of the places that carries cannon-like pressure. In the case of this wave, Mark Healey is looking at section number two.

CRAZY WILL DILLON

If anyone has charged Puerto harder than anybody—with brash, sometimes peculiar bravado, willing to take mega risks to get the enormous barrel he wants—it's Will Dillon. Every one knows him as Crazy Will, his handle since he began surfing Puerto in the early 2000s. Earning a nickname like "Crazy Will," amongst a contingent of big-wave surfers whose sanity is often in question, indicates his nature as a next-level charger.

During his early excursions to Puerto, Dillon quickly wrangled everybody's attention. He made giant tubes, took radical spills, and, wildest of all, pulled into closeouts on thirty-foot-plus waves—waves not one other person in the water would ever consider. His simple motivation was to get enormous tubes, and he was always ready to deal with the consequences.

But he can take a beating. He's a tough, rugged guy: a hardcore spear fisherman, a bit of a maniac on his motorcycle, which he occasionally crashes, and never scared of a fight. He takes beatings, but always comes up solid and shrugs them off. None of them has slowed him down; he's still living in Puerto with his local wife and kids, waiting for the heaviest days, when he paddles out on his nine-foot-six with no leash or flotation, whips it on the biggest waves, and locks himself into the Crazy Will tubes he loves—closeout or no, he'll go.

Dillon's part in Nigel Devenport's recent surf film *Nature of the Beast* reveals his unique passion and unwavering gumption. One section ends with Dillon, the solo paddle surfer out on a dark, foreboding, enormous day, taking a particularly nasty closeout. It's a Crazy Will wave—huge and unmakeable. Leashless, he loses his board, swims in casually in a far-from-casual situation, strolls up the beach in his typical, nonchalant fashion, and offers Devenport a play-by-play. "I didn't know if it was going to close out," he explains, "but when I saw it was going to, I rode up about halfway to avoid the massive lip coming over. I got in the gas chamber and the mist just put me to sleep like a baby. Nothing special—but hey, there was a moment there."

It's those "moments" that Crazy Will lives for. In pursuing them he's become synonymous with big Puerto over the last decade, one of the true characters in Puerto's ever-evolving lineage.

LEFT: Will Dillon only surfs when it's big, and then only looks for the biggest ones. He's been a classic fixture in Puerto since the early 2000s.

WAIMEA BAY

WAIMEA BAY, on Oahu's North Shore, is where big-wave surfing began. The bravado that drove early legends like Greg Noll, Pat Curren, and George Downing to surf big Waimea in the 1950s has inspired and influenced big-wave surfers of every generation.

Both the Waimea Bay and Waimea Valley have long been held sacred by Hawaiians. Fresh water flows from the valley; the bay offers easy accessibility in and out of the ocean (except during the largest winter swells); and the area is the site of one of largest religious ceremonial grounds in the Hawaiian Islands, the Pu'u o Mahuka Heiau. Potent, sacred energy imbues the entire area, transcending into modern-day surfing and oceangoing culture at the Bay.

Waimea was long the place against which all big-wave discoveries were measured. Then, in the '90s, interest in Oahu's outer reefs and the pioneering of Maui's Peahi (or Jaws) set a new scale. But Waimea remains an important proving ground. Here, most Hawaiians and visiting surfers get their start and develop enough skill and confidence to move on to other big-wave lineups. And every few years, on giant swells, the Bay comes alive and hosts amazing gatherings of people—particularly when the legendary Eddie Aikau event is held.

OPPOSITE: Waimea Bay from above.

TOP: *Hokule'a* entering the Bay during the opening ceremony of the Eddie.

BOTTOM: Paying respect at the opening ceremony for the Eddie.

EDDIE WOULD GO

The Quiksilver in Memory of Eddie Aikau, typically referred to simply as the Eddie, is the most prestigious surf event in the world. Every year, the legendary North Shore lifeguard is celebrated with this memorial event, and the message of his values and way of life is shared with the surfing world. It is a tradition unmatched in the sport—and an annual reminder to live more like Eddie, who was positive, humble, giving, selfless, courageous, and inspirational. He embodied the spirit of the Hawaiian waterman—saving people in the ocean, partaking in all manner of ocean activities, and riding the biggest waves that Waimea Bay had to offer.

Aikau disappeared at sea on March 17, 1978, attempting to save the lives of fellow sailors on board the *Hokule'a*, a Polynesian voyaging canoe, shortly after it set off to Tahiti and ran into problems. Aikau abandoned the boat and set out toward shore to get help. He was never seen again. But his legend brings people together in a celebration of life and the sea, and when the day calls for it, those who have followed in his footsteps ride amazing waves in his honor.

To earn spots on the Eddie's list of twenty-four invitees and twenty-four alternates, surfers must dedicate themselves to big-wave surfing and earn the respect of their peers for doing so. It is the greatest honor in big-wave surfing to make this list and partake in the process of passing along Eddie's ideals. The event is greatly anticipated and held only when the waves are forty-plus feet, which has happened only eight times since the Eddie's inception in 1987. It takes a very special day for Waimea Bay to be deemed Eddie-worthy—and for the 2009 event, special it was.

The Eddie's annual opening ceremony happens at the beginning of a winter-long

RIGHT: Shane Dorian and Mark Healey on one of the biggest waves ridden at the Bay in modern times. It was the evening before the 2009 Eddie event, and while most other competitors had retired for the day, these two were looking for a giant. It was getting late and according to Healey most were ready to go in. "At that point, I made up my mind thinking, 'I can't be out here 'til dark. I've got to surf the event tomorrow. Next big wave that comes in, I don't care what it looks like, I'm going.' And it just happened to be that wave. I turned around, put my head down, and paddled as hard as I could. I remember almost pearling at the top but somehow stuck in and got off the bottom and that's when I actually looked over to my right, and I saw Shane. Not only did I not see him paddling for the wave because I had my blinders on, but I was surprised somebody else tried to go for it, really. I'm happy Shane caught that wave too, because that's obviously the best vindication that you could have. I talked to him about it, and he said, 'That's one of the biggest waves I have ever caught.'"

waiting period. At the start of December 2009, those invited gathered at the Bay for the ceremony and rumor had it that the Eddie might run just a few days later. El Niño winter was in full swing, and a massive storm was developing that had all the trappings to create an "Eddie swell." It was big enough, it was close enough, and the vibe was there. The North Shore was abuzz with anticipation.

The day before the contest was the biggest day in years—but local weather and a slow rise in the swell through the morning put the contest on hold. By the afternoon, though, rogue forty- to fifty-foot waves were unloading at the Bay, and many of the competitors got in the water. Some wanted to get reacquainted with the lineup, feel it out, maybe snag a few, and get into a rhythm—hopefully without taking a big wipeout. Others saw the afternoon as an opportunity to catch the biggest wave Waimea Bay was capable of holding.

Mark Healey and Shane Dorian fell into the second category, being committed guys who're always looking for the biggest, heaviest waves of the day. As the horizon went black with swell, nearly everyone in the lineup paddled out to the safety of deep water, hoping to avoid the dark, feathering horizon, but Healey and Dorian held position, both intent on riding the wave.

It reached the lineup, every bit of fifty feet, raw and thick. They muscled into it—arguably one of the biggest waves ridden at the Bay. They were about fifteen feet apart from each other, in their own worlds, not even aware they were both on the wave until it was well over and they'd resurfaced after the avalanche of white-water had mowed them down.

After that afternoon, anticipation levels overflowed for the next day, which was predicted to be slightly smaller, but much cleaner. Morning dawned to the cracking of big waves and ocean mist in the air. The swell had

cleaned up and gone pristine, as predicted. It was a dreamy North Shore day: light winds, beaming sun, and perfect Waimea.

Over the years at the Eddie, certain people have fallen into a rhythm and had everything come together. It's commonly said that Eddie chooses these people, and that a deeper, almost spiritual element is a factor in who finds the flow. The inaugural winner at the Bay was Eddie's younger brother Clyde Aikau in 1986; in 1990 it was Keone Downing, son of big-wave pioneer George Downing, though Brock Little also put on a legendary performance. In 1999 it was Noah Johnson; Australian Ross Clarke-Jones took it in 2001; professional surfing legend Kelly Slater won in 2002; and Bruce Irons won in 2004.

THESE PAGES: True Hawaiian heavyweights: Kala Alexander (below) and Sunny Garcia (opposite).

In the 2009 event, Kelly Slater, the best surfer in the world, seemed about to become the first two-time winner. In his masterful fashion, he went into his first round and effortlessly dominated, running far enough into the lead with his scores that an unprecedented second win seemed likely.

As the day wore on, it looked like Slater had it in the bag. He was far in the lead with his four accumulated scores over two rounds of surfing, and leading up to the last heat of the day, nobody had caught up to him. Only Bruce Irons looked to have a chance, but it would be a hefty task. All the others in the final heat would need near-miracles to win.

Greg, surfing in his first Eddie, never gave up hope. He'd had a shocker of a first round and didn't have a score worth keeping; for his hour-long final heat, he would need four high-scoring waves. Competitors are only allowed to ride four waves per heat, so Greg couldn't miss a beat: he couldn't fall, and every wave had to be solid. Practically speaking, he was out of contention.

Still, Greg had won a number of big-wave contests, and he was determined. "I was sitting in next-to-last place, but I never once doubted

that I could still win," he later reflected. "Doing so was obviously going to be a lot tougher. I needed to ride four outstanding waves. But with the biggest sets of the day starting to march into the Bay, I knew I could still do it."

As soon as the last heat hit the water, those big sets began pulsing in, faster than they had the entire day. Everybody in the heat traded incredible waves. Sunny Garcia had a couple of beauties. Ramon Navarro nailed a perfect score for the biggest wave of the day. And Greg found the exact rhythm he needed.

His first wave was good—not a giant score, but it got him started. He got back outside, and one of the biggest waves of the day came to him—a gift he rode from the most critical point, earning a perfect score that put him back in the mix. He got back out, and sure enough, there was another incredible wave for him. This time it was a heavy, technical drop, and he did an amazing job of keeping his weight back and not burying the board. It was another high score, and suddenly he was back in play. One more decent wave and he would be the winner.

Time was winding down. Greg had passed up a couple waves he didn't want. And then it came to him: a nice midsized set that

let him down the face smoothly for a solid—yet not too risky—ride. The score came in: it was enough. He'd won in four waves, in the last heat of the day. It was an astonishing feat. The sequence of events really made it feel like Eddie had an idea of what he wanted that day, guiding Greg to a pinnacle event of his life.

"I will always acknowledge winning the Eddie as my greatest surfing achievement, and my performance that day as the best of my life," explained Greg. "Not necessarily the way I surfed, but rather my mindset and mental outlook going into it. Winning the Eddie was one of my childhood dreams, and my sense of elation and accomplishment afterwards was unparalleled—and it will probably remain that way. Afterwards, when I actually had time to reflect on the entire day and experience, I came to realize what was most special about the experience was not actually the winning, but rather the memories, friendships, and blessings I'd encountered on my journey towards achieving that goal. Those moments were the real gift in it all."

As of 2015, the Eddie has yet to run again.

ABOVE: Kelly Slater heading out for the Eddie
opening ceremony.

OPPOSITE: Kelly Slater took his everyday prowess
to the Bay this day and looked generally unbeatable.
Ultimately he was runner-up.

THESE PAGES: Greg Long surfed four consecutive waves to victory during the last heat of the day, which saw a spike in the swell. A triumphant combination of lucky timing, total preparation, and a never-give-up attitude saw him to the winner's podium.

ABOVE: Kohl Christensen has charged the outer reefs as hard as anyone, ever. This is pre-safety days when surfing in trunks was the norm, and water safety was nonexistent aside from your surfing partners.

OPPOSITE TOP: Mike Pietsch, part of a devout underground crew of North Shore chargers, locked into the outer-reef wilderness of Himalayas.

OAHU'S OUTER REEFS

IT IS NO SURPRISE that Oahu's intimidating outer reefs—with names like Himalayas, Phantoms, and Alligators—command the utmost respect from the tight-knit posses who've ridden them for years. The name of a surf spot creates an air around it, as evidenced by the foreboding Jaws, Dungeons, and Killers; Oahu's outer reefs are no exception.

On a fabled stretch of coastline boasting more big-wave lore and heavy-water breaks than any other, these outer reefs represent the biggest challenge. Breaking nearly a mile out offshore, these waves have power and consequence without parallel. World-class big-wave surfer Todd Chesser perished in 1997 at Outside Alligator's, as did Kirk Passmore in 2013—evidence of the gravity of these surfing venues.

These reefs are the final frontier on the North Shore—and they're the only options when swells reach XXL proportions and the entire coastline is a relentless, unrideable wash of ocean fury. On the rare days that are so big even Waimea can't handle the swell, the outer reefs are at their best. The bigger they get, the better they get, and on such days a small pack of the most committed chargers in the world step into the oceanic wilderness and hunt these moving monuments.

Over the last decade, the biggest self-powered sessions have gone down at Himalayas, a left-hand beast outside and west of Laniakea. In prime form, its massive walls of water ledge with incredible power and turn into giant tubing waves, capable of producing the ride of a lifetime.

For years, a network of chargers, led by Kohl Christensen, Mark Healey, Dave Wassel, Mike Stewart, and a handful of underground characters, pursued these massive waves for nothing more than the love. They kept their sessions discreet and themselves anonymous, not wanting to attract attention to these outer-water sanctuaries where they could do what they loved without the crowds of Waimea Bay. For Christensen, surfing Himalayas represented the ultimate test of big-wave dedication. "Being out there by yourself with a huge set approaching and having to decide whether or not you're gonna go is the most exhilarating feeling in the world," he explains. "No cameras, no peers watching, just you and the wave. That's when you figure out why you are really doing it, or if you even want to be doing it."

Those who've ridden these reefs in the purest, simplest form animatedly recount stories of survival. No Jet Skis, no flotation devices, questionable leashes—but nobody cared in those days. It was get yourself out, get yourself in. Long swims resulting from broken boards and leashes were the norm, top fitness an absolute requisite—and your fellow surfers were your only safety net. It just doesn't get any more hardcore.

HARD TO HIDE
AN ELEPHANT

It was the El Niño winter of 2009–'10 when Himalayas finally emerged in the media, and for understandable reasons. Hawaii was getting pounded by giant swells, and the waves being ridden were simply too magnificent to go undocumented. Meanwhile, the greater surfing public was experiencing renewed interest in self-powered big-wave surfing.

A few images from the first sessions of that winter circulated around the mainstream media, to great awe. Suddenly, Himalayas was a big-wave epicenter. The number of new surfers riding the reef increased exponentially as the season wore on. It was a new situation out there. And while crowds can make things difficult, they can also prompt an elevation in performance—especially when Jet Ski safety and documentation find their way into the mix.

Sion Milosky was one individual who had the determination, skill, and passion to take paddling giant waves further—and he used Himalayas as his platform to show the world what was possible. A gifted surfer, with the knack of getting the day's best waves anywhere he surfed, Sion had a humble, low-key approach, a quiet warrior who always played at the highest level of risk and reward. This was his year. Everywhere he surfed that winter, he rode the biggest, best waves. People have periods in their surfing lives when everything clicks: their boards are right, their fitness and mindspace are honed, and they're tapped into the greater flow of things. That's where Sion was. His flow culminated in the biggest publicly documented paddle-in wave anybody had ever seen attempted at the time—an absolute giant, somewhere above sixty feet and carrying every ounce of potential heaviness with it. He ultimately came unglued about halfway down—the velocity got too great—but his heroic effort upped the ante of what was possible. It was a milestone.

THESE PAGES: Sion Milosky on one of the biggest waves ever paddled into during the 2009/10 El Niño winter. As Kohl Christensen remarked of Sion, "The two years before he passed I got to witness another level of determination in a human being. He had a fire in him unparalleled to anything I've seen, combined with incredible skill and courage."

HEALEY'S OUTER REEF TALE

Over the last decade, Mark Healey—one of the North Shore's most fearless, confident, and dedicated watermen—has seen more days at Himalayas than most, and he knows what the place is capable of. One day in particular—during which he was left out by himself after sunset—is etched in his mind.

"It was more than a decade ago now," Healey recounted on a quiet North Shore afternoon in 2014. "It was just Dave Wassel and me out there at Himalayas. It was amazing: twenty feet solid, the way we call it here—so forty-plus feet on the face. The swell was rising, so there was a lot of inertia and water behind it, and Himalayas was drawing it in and really doing it right—long, top-to-bottom barrels, like having three different Pipelines stacked next to each other at twenty feet. Just incredible!

"It was already pretty scary, and the swell just kept ratcheting up and up. Every set was getting bigger and bigger, and we were just barely scratching over them every time. As it got later, we started figuring that it might be time to catch a wave in and get out of there before dark.

"It was huge by then. I had never seen waves that big up to that point, and the amount of water it was drawing off the reef enabled us to actually see the contour of the ledge of the reef sucking down below sea level—the same way you can see that lump in front of the wave at Teahupo'o. And it was doing the same kind of things you see at Teahupo'o, like six-second-long spits—just absolutely radical stuff going on.

"It was cat and mouse. The normal sets were bigger than any waves I had ever caught before, and the big sets—well, it wasn't even crossing my mind to turn around and try to paddle for one. This is still back when we were both in board shorts. We weren't even wearing spring suits. Back then, if you wore a suit you were considered a pussy—and personal flotation wasn't even in the picture yet. So we're in board shorts—no suits, no flotation, no one on a Jet Ski watching us, not even a chance anyone could see us out there from land—it's getting late, and the swell is just ratcheting up and up. After seeing similar-size waves since then, I'd say it was thirty feet solid; what I would consider

RIGHT: Mark Healey has a distinct relationship and comfort level at Himalayas acquired by growing up there and surfing it a lot. He sits deep, and picks the thickest of waves, keenly looking for the ones that really tube. There are only a few people doing that.

THESE PAGES: Healey with a little
head wound to tighten some screws.

thirty feet. It was bigger than anything that
anybody's paddled into at Jaws so far, for sure.
Significantly bigger.

"So we're just cat-and-mousing, trying to
get a wave in, and this average-size set, which
is twenty, twenty-five feet, comes in. Wassel was
on an eleven-foot board, and as we're paddling
out, he just turns around and whips it. I'm
looking down and I can see the contour of the
reef sucking off, and the only thing I could get
out of my mouth was 'I can't save you!' I yelled it
out. That's all I told him. That's the only thing that
came to my head. 'I just hope you're not making
this decision based on me being able to help
you out, because we're utterly lost out here,' I
was thinking.

"And this is after he had already broken his
leash. Earlier in the session, he had broken his
leash, and his board went sixty yards in from
us into the impact zone, but somehow it shot up
out of the whitewater. He had fallen on the drop
or bailed or something, and he looks at me, and
says, 'Get it for me, please!' I thought, 'Are you
fucking kidding me right now? I gotta go paddle

sixty yards into the impact zone between sets,
and it's like thirty feet right now?' I ended up
doing it. Paddled as fast as I could in and got
it, put his leash in my teeth, and fricking raced
back out. Got his board to him, then we kept
paddling out and just barely made it over the
next set. Get this—then he took the two pieces
of his leash and tied it in an overhand knot in
the middle, thinking that it was going to make a
difference of some sort, right?

"So that's the backstory to him whipping on
this wave that was a fucked-up, radical, radical
wave. And all I can say is, 'I can't save you!' And
I'll never forget the view—it's the same view
that I had when Andy Irons caught that crazy
wave at Teahupo'o that he side-slipped into. I
was looking down that wave the same way I was
looking down Wassel's wave. In both situations,
it looked like the wave was already barreling
over them before they stood up. I thought, 'No
way he made it to his feet. That was just suicide.
Not a chance.'

"So I watched this wave, thinking, 'God,
this is bad.' It would unload a giant section,

"THE SUN WAS SETTING, AND I THOUGHT, 'I HAVE TO FORCE THE ISSUE. I'VE GOT TO DO THIS OUT OF SURVIVAL . . .'"

blow guts for like three seconds, go into a second section, blow guts, and then right when the third section was coming, Wassel punches through the back with his hands out, screaming, 'Yeeaaaahh!'

"The other thing we were doing that day—something we used to do—was see who could keep their dip in the longest. So he's screaming, 'Yeeeaaaahh!' and gets sucked back over and then comes up, still screaming, 'Yeeeaaaahhh!' pulls his dip out of his mouth, and just starts swimming in.

"'Oh my god! I hope you make it in,' I thought—because he was so far down the line on the wave, and you don't want to get close to that channel, because the rip just nukes between there and Laniakea. I was just hoping he was able to edge into the impact zone and get pushed in.

"Wassel will tell you this story, too. He's no stranger to telling tall tales, but I have to validate this one, because there's no way he could have ridden that wave and gotten to that point where he was without being absolutely kegged the whole time—on an eleven-foot board, just pig-dogging.

"So that happened, and then I was stuck out there by myself. And it was still getting bigger and bigger and nearing sunset. I remember just barely getting over these waves that were the biggest, greenest walls I'd ever seen. It was nuts. So I'm cat-and-mousing the whole time, trying to catch one without getting caught inside. As I was paddling over one wave, there were a bunch of those needlefish that you've got to watch out for when they jump. So as I was paddling over this thirty-footer that was going top to bottom, barely making it, these needlefish were chasing other bait through the wall of the wave. One almost hit me in the eye, so I had to roll over my board, and almost got sucked over the falls because of it. I thought, "Oh my god, I'm feeling really uncomfortable. I need to leave. This is an omen.'

"The sun was setting, and I thought, 'I have to force the issue. I've got to do this out of survival and whip on something.' Finally, one of the 'normal' sets came, which was big. And I ended up whipping on it, and it felt like I took two drops; I'd never been on a wave that big before, and I actually pulled in and got a barrel. I rode it all the way in and it was just getting dark when I hit the beach. Wassel was in there doing jumping jacks, he was so pumped.

"It felt so good to get to the beach. I have a never-say-die attitude, but I knew if I was still out after dark, I was in deep shit. I was thinking I would just have to paddle straight out to sea and weather the night out, because if you got caught and broke your leash and were swimming and got stuck in that rip and recycled, you'd be fucked. I'd have had better odds just keeping my board and going out to sea. So I had to catch that last wave.

"That was an intense experience. I don't know if I'll ever see it like that out there again."

JAWS

OFF MAUI'S NORTH SHORE, Peahi, commonly known as Jaws, is the ultimate big-wave arena. Those that have tested their skills and limits in the lineup—nearly all the best in the world—agree on this. It is on the grandest scale of size, heaviness, and power in which the notorious horseshoe-shaped bowls unload over the massive boulders, which seem to have been auspiciously placed to compose this perfect reef. This is the king of waves.

Since Jaws's inception as a surf spot, dedicated, highly skilled individuals have developed intimate bonds with the place. Jaws's early years as the world's foremost tow-surfing venue—pioneered by Laird Hamilton, Darrick Doerner, Dave Kalama, and a passionate crew of others based on Maui during the '90s and into the early 2000s—was an incomparable time in big-wave history. It was the beginning of tow surfing and ushered in a new realm of wave size. The arena provided a perfect—and enormous—canvas on which to experiment and progress, and Laird and crew shattered boundaries with the Jet Ski assist, completely redefining the way in which people could approach and ride giant waves.

These early glory years of Jaws and tow surfing—when this skilled group rode amazing waves with no one else around—is a moment in surfing that can never be replicated. As documentation of the pioneers' adventures circulated, the popularity of tow surfing boomed, and every winter more and more teams showed up at Jaws. By 2004, tow surfing had gotten out of control. There were so many Jet Skis in the lineup at Jaws that order and etiquette disappeared. People vied for the same waves, got in one another's way, and marred the lineup with ski wakes. The number of tow teams exceeded what the lineup could handle, and the camaraderie so unique to big-wave surfing was harder to find, often replaced by frustration.

Truth is, tow surfing was just too accessible. Anybody who wanted to tow into a wave could; gone were the nuances of positioning and tracking down a wave, as well as the fear of getting caught inside—perhaps the most terrifying aspect of big-wave surfing. People were towing waves who weren't capable of paddling, and the lineup was riddled with inexperienced riders. Jaws itself seemed to acknowledge this: After one giant day in 2004, when enormous waves were ridden amid a huge crowd, it receded into a much-needed, rarely interrupted slumber with few giant days.

Between 2004 and 2014, though, a pursuit previously considered unlikely developed. People had long mused about the possibility of paddling Jaws, but the general consensus was that it wasn't approachable. "Too much wind, too much water moving too fast, and waves too big to catch" were common excuses. The points of reference for this analysis were the giant days, when tow teams gathered to catch the biggest, heaviest waves—the ones truly too big to paddle. But there were other days out there—days in the thirty- to fifty-foot range—where tow surfing was actually slightly unimpressive. The big-wave paddle renaissance was flourishing, and many started to reassess Jaws's paddle potential.

LEFT: The North Shore's Makua Rothman, weightless and about to pick up serious velocity on one of the biggest, cleanest waves to ever get paddled into and ridden to completion at Jaws during the historic October 7, 2012, session.

ABOVE: The arena at Jaws.

THESE PAGES: Laird Hamilton (right) and Garrett McNamara (above), at the peak of tow surfing mania in 2004 (top). They are two of the dominant alpha figures who led the charge in the lineup, always riding the biggest, best waves in the most critical manner—examples of tow surfing at its highest level.

RELEARNING

Over the winters of 2007 through 2009, a handful of Brazilian surfers living in the Hawaiian Islands, including Yuri Soledade, Danilo Couto, and Marcio Freire, began paddling some of Jaws's smaller days, riding the lefts off the peak. This sparked intrigue in others, and during the winter of 2010–'11, paddling at Jaws kicked into a higher gear. Some of the best big-wave riders in the world made their virgin pilgrimage to this mecca of massive surf—this time to take on the rights, the hallmark of Jaws.

On February 8, 2011, Healey, Greg, Ian Walsh, and Danilo Couto partnered up and gave the rights their first real dig. Couto had a couple of years of experience at Jaws already, and nailed the wave of the day: a heavy right off the peak, beginning with an airdrop and ending with an intense pocket ride. It later earned him Ride of the Year at the Billabong XXL Awards. The others had memorable waves, too, and the session inspired everyone present to take paddling Jaws to the next level.

TOP: It is a large playing field to paddle amongst, and cleanup sets are regular, especially on the bigger days, making them all the scarier.

ABOVE: Danilo Cuoto (left) and Nathan Fletcher (right).

OPPOSITE: Danilo Cuoto, one of the early paddle pioneers at Jaws, as centered and poised as possible, hoping the wind does not lift the nose of the board any higher and rip it away—a common occurrence with all the wind up the face at Jaws, and the cause of many radical wipeouts.

On March 15, 2011, another opportunity to paddle Jaws arose, and it would likely be the last of the season. Shane Dorian, who had missed the previous session, was ready for this one, and he, Ian Walsh, and a handful of others paddled out. Thirty- to sixty-foot waves were squaring up on the reef under difficult, blustery wind conditions, but these guys dug in and charged with vigor.

This session began Dorian's legendary, triumphant relationship with Jaws. He rode the biggest wave of the day—an ultra-steep drop that fed him into a massive tube—and set a lofty new standard. At fifty-seven feet, the wave set a new world record at the time for the biggest paddle wave ever documented, and the tube factor distinguished the ride. The big-wave world was dumbfounded. The ante had been upped.

Entering this new, consequential territory further catalyzed the movement toward greater safety measures. Dorian worked with Billabong to develop the first inflatable wetsuits. Group training sessions to develop lifesaving skill sets were organized by Kohl Christensen and Couto, and as safety precautions increased, so too did the level of big-wave surfing.

Since that February 2011 session, Jaws has become the preeminent venue for redefining the possibilities of self-powered big-wave surfing. A new generation of young Maui chargers—led by Billy Kemper, Albee Layer, DK, Shaun, and Ian Walsh, and Kai Lenny—are growing up with Jaws as their wave, collectively deciphering just how to approach it. Experienced veterans like Dorian, Healey, Greg, Wassel, Twiggy, Makua Rothman, and others are getting the waves of their lives. More surfers show up to every session properly equipped. As history repeats itself at Jaws—in the more primal discipline of man, board, and wave—we will continue seeing feats of bravery and brilliance.

THESE PAGES: Shane Dorian and a fifty-seven-foot tube ride on March 15, 2011. Up to this point the rights had only been flirted with. This wave set the lofty standard of what can be done paddle surfing at Jaws.

THESE PAGES: As a lifelong big-wave specialist and North Shore lifeguard, Dave Wassel has had more time in Hawaii's power than anybody else of this generation. He is one of a small handful of people who would attempt a paddle wave this size at Jaws, and of the even fewer who could have gotten down the face before getting annihilated at the bottom. It doesn't get any heavier or more committed than this ride. Wassel recounts the session: "That day was chaotic. Alex Gray and I repelled down a muddy cliff toting ten-and-a-half-foot surfboards. Before jumping off the rocks, I watched a wave explode on the shore and blow Kohl Christensen one hundred yards back up the river. Another wave destroyed four other surfers and their boards on the rocks. It was just crazy, and we were still on the shore. I'm actually afraid of heights, and I blank out on most of my big wave rides. I remember the loud explosion as the wave gobbled me up. I remember my ears popping five to six times as I was forced down into the darkness. I remember my board hitting me in the thigh and I remember pulling the cord on my inflation vest so hard that I broke the cord and handle clean off."

MAUI GLASS

Maui is notoriously windy, and that wind presented challenges during most of the paddle sessions that went down between 2007 and 2011. The persistent 20-mph side-shore trade winds made it difficult to catch and get down the face of the waves, causing many radical wipeouts. A big day without wind was the common dream among the area's hard-charging crew. It would make life so much easier and it was bound to happen at some point, though glassy days on Maui are a rarity. "Fifteen-mph trades is Maui glass," explains Maui local Ian Walsh, laughing.

That day came on October 9, 2012—early in the season for a swell of consequence. A wave hadn't broken along the reef for half a year, and as the reality of the swell came to fruition, it appeared something special was lining up, grabbing the attention of everybody interested in paddling Jaws. Boards were pulled from their storage spots as preparation for a real-deal session commenced.

The elements came together. An ideal north-northwest swell made for forty- to fifty-foot-plus waves, kissed with light offshore winds. Ravenous but surprisingly surfable tubes spun down the reef. Healey was among the crew who experienced the rare Maui glass. "It was night and day how approachable the waves were," he says. "Just an average wave that comes in on a windy day is such a challenge. The wind makes it so difficult, but on a glassy day like that you could paddle into the eighteen-footers easily. Twenty-footers took some effort—and then the

big ones really took some effort, but were still approachable. It makes a world of difference. Everybody had been dreaming of a day when there wouldn't be wind chop to contend with. And that was it."

Enough people had amassed for the rare conditions that a supersession element came into play; nearly everybody in the water got an insane wave. Greg, Healey, Walsh, Rothman, and Layer scored beauties, but it was Dorian—once again—who was the standout, putting it all on the line without missing a beat or making a mistake. The session further cemented his legacy as the most committed big-wave surfer of this generation—perhaps ever. His final wave of the day will always be referenced among the best rides of all time.

That particular wave came late in the afternoon. The swell was rising, and he and Healey were left in the lineup. Dorian saw the set stacking from a long way out. Rather than paddle for the horizon—as many would have—he held position until the giant wave came to him. He paddled like a machine on his ten-foot-six and got to his feet with a clean entrance. The wave looked approachable at first, but intensified quickly: the wave bottomed out, and churned up a car-sized boil. Once beyond the boil, he set his bottom turn, and the wave corkscrewed onto the reef. He set his line, stood up tall, hands above his head momentarily, and drove through a meaty Jaws tube that eventually spit him out into the channel. History made.

RIGHT Shane Dorian locked in the guts of arguably the best paddle ride to date at Jaws.

PAGES 122–123: Mark Healey on an absolute monster. "Toward the end of the day, the swell started ratcheting up, and I knew there were going to be opportunities. Only Dorian and I were left out there, and these big sets were coming, so I thought, 'Okay, now's my time to try to get a real big one.' I got this wave, and it was so doubled up that I knew it was going to turn into a mutant. I was out in the flats and realized I couldn't get under the lip so the last second I decided to straighten out. I thought the lip was going to land on me but it just landed on my heels, thank God. It was a foot and a half away from a direct hit on my shoulders. It was one of the worst, most violent beatings I've ever had in my life."

THESE PAGES: Two hungry forces of Maui's young paddle
contingent: Matt Meola (above) and Billy Kemper (opposite).

IAN WALSH ON JAWS

Growing up on Maui, Ian Walsh was surrounded by the lore of Jaws. He started towing there with Shane Dorian at an early age and quickly gained a reputation as one of the heaviest young guns in the lineup. When momentum shifted toward paddling at Jaws, Walsh was instrumental—especially in the early investigation of the rights. His dedication advanced the movement and inspired other top big-wave surfers to give the lineup a go. He's taken a captain's role and he and his brothers DK and Shaun have helped facilitate the venue's paddle sessions, and have proved valuable guides for surfers from around the world. Walsh has been a staple in the lineup, figuring out the possibilities (and impossibilities), hanging in the pit, and charging with high skill and calculated abandon.

RL: What was it like, growing up on Maui and watching Jaws during such a monumental era in big-wave history?

IAN WALSH: When I was really young, I don't think I was quite able to process what was happening

out there. I remember surfing a little reform in a tucked-away cove during a massive swell about eight miles away from Jaws, and I found one of the guys' tow boards that had washed in on the rocks. I remember trying to visualize how big it must have been to push the board that far away that quickly. Seeing some of those tow days, along with some of the old Eddie events when I was young, helped leave a little mark in the back of my mind—visualizing and dreaming about riding waves that big.

RL: When did you know you wanted to surf Jaws?

IAN WALSH: We have such a huge variety—from reefs, points, and sandbars to slabs and big-wave spots. So when I was a little kid, I would get to see Jaws from the cliff, but I was pretty consumed with surfing a few other waves around the island that were good on the same swells. Until the first time I rode a wave at Jaws, I always wondered why the guys out there would spend so much time there on the biggest swells, when other waves on Maui were as good as they get.

TOP: Ian Walsh on the type of wave that gives the break its name.

ABOVE: Walsh prepping his Jaws quiver.

OPPOSITE: The Walsh Brothers: DK, Ian, and Shaun.

But I got into surfing bigger waves when Matt Kinoshita pushed me into going out with him on big days to some of the other outer reefs on Maui. I was about fourteen or so. Just being out on some of those swells—even though I was scared and would sit on the shoulder—started my wheels turning. I decided I didn't want to miss any big days. A few years later—when I was about sixteen or seventeen—I decided I wanted to surf Jaws. My neighbor Luke Hargreaves used to tow into Jaws all the time, and one day when I was heading out to catch the bus to school, I saw him getting his Jet Ski and gear ready for a surf out there, and he invited me to come when I got back. School wrapped up, and I got home and jotted down a quick note to my mom, letting her know I went surfing, then took off. As soon as I dropped into my first wave out there, I understood why you would want to be out there every swell—there was nowhere else on the planet to be! That single wave left a mark on me forever. All I wanted to do was get a bigger one, or ride the next one a little bit deeper and push myself further. I rode about five waves that day, on a weighted six-foot-ten [board] with two big fins close to each other on each side of the stringer. Shortly after that, Ahanu Tson-Dru and I borrowed an old beat-up Jet Ski and started heading out on every swell.

RL: Which sessions have been the most memorable?

IAN WALSH: Tow-in was January 10, 2004. I think those were the biggest waves I have ever seen consistently come through all day. Every set came with so much energy, and one rogue set at the peak of the day came through that hit a different part of the reef and was bigger than anything I have ever seen out there.

Paddle-in was February 8, 2011. This was the first time a few of us had given the right a decent go on swell with a lot of power. That day really opened my eyes to what was achievable, paddling out there.

RL: You have been at the forefront of paddle-surfing Jaws. Do you think the paddle approach can go much further, beyond what's been achieved out there?

IAN WALSH: What makes surfing so fun is that there is no out-of-bounds line. With big waves, the approachability when it gets really solid depends a lot on the type of conditions the swells come with. I think every aspect of surfing can go well beyond what has already been achieved, paddling big waves included. The natural evolution will lead the next generation to push beyond what's happening at the moment. Their creativity and desire to push themselves past what they know and what they have seen will keep the evolution of our sport moving into very exciting places.

RL: Have you ever paddle-surfed anywhere else that has the intensity of Jaws?

IAN WALSH: I think all the major big-wave zones feel intense on the right days. It's all positioning; you're either on a three-foot triangle that's giving you a launch ramp into the wave, or you're not. If you have that window into the wave it all comes down to feeling: if you're feeling it, then it's time to send it.

RL: Shane Dorian has been your main surfing partner over the years, so you've been front seat to his mind-blowing feats. Do you think we'll ever see anybody else reach that level?

IAN WALSH: I have learned a ton from Shane, in and out of the water, over the years I have been so fortunate to spend with him. He is a very special surfer. I think we will see people reach that level and it will definitely be a testament to what he has done—he's the one helping others visualize what's possible.

RL: What have been your best personal moments out there?

IAN WALSH: It is really hard to narrow down all the sessions we have had out there into a few moments. I think watching how far my brothers have progressed in big waves out there is definitely one of them. More than anything, I am just psyched to have a wave of that caliber in my backyard—I know it's there, and that it will always present opportunities for me to push myself as far as I want to go.

RL: And scariest?

IAN WALSH: There have been a few, and there will be a few more. But one stands out to me still, ten years later. On January 10, 2004, I took a wave where I was a little bit deep, and tried to pull into the pocket of the wave to make it. It clamped and landed straight on my chest, blowing my life jacket zipper right apart and knocking the wind out of me as I penetrated the water. Then I felt the weightless feeling as the wave lifted me up towards the lip, as I made my way over what felt like a fifty-foot waterfall, followed by pure violence. After trying to work my way to the surface through the turbulence—while barely hanging on to my life jacket that was now wrapped around my face and shoulders—the need for air really set in. I was swimming as hard as I could to get to the surface, then all of a sudden, as the urge to breathe became worse and worse, my arms and legs just stopped working. I can vividly remember telling myself to kick with my legs and pull with my arms, but my body had shut everything down to conserve oxygen for my brain (what I learned much later). Being completely lucid and knowing I needed to swim, but was unable to, was really scary. Then, in a last-second panic, I opened my eyes to gauge how far I was from the surface, and all I saw was black. It should have been white or blue, from how close I was to the surface. I later learned I may have been in the process of blacking out. Then, less than a second later, I popped up and got a breath, just before another really big wave hit me and sent me straight back down. That air was enough for me to compose myself and ride out the next beating, then slowly swim my way toward the inside. I don't think I will ever forget that.

SOUTH PACIFIC

L

ike its counterpart to the north, the South Pacific is one of the broadest, most diverse swaths of ocean in the world. From the tropical tube-riding venues of Tahiti and Fiji to the cold, formidable coast of Chile, the region is blessed with consistent surf and frequently clean conditions due to the ocean's expansiveness and the great distant swells often travel before they reach key big-wave locations.

The swell-producing storms of the South Pacific typically form along the coast of Antarctica before tracking northward. Storms develop quickly in these extreme southern waters, then take particular trajectories, depending on how the dominant high pressures over the South Pacific are situated. Some swell and high-pressure patterns send surf directly to the Polynesian islands throughout the Pacific. Others track east and send surf directly to South America. And as with the North Pacific, the occasional storm will traverse the entire South Pacific and send surf to the Pacific Islands, South America, and on up to Central and North America. Regardless of a storm's specific trajectory, it is rarely quiet in the South Pacific from April through October.

Tahiti and Fiji (with Teahupo'o and Cloudbreak as the premier waves in each island chain, respectively) have played a significant role in the progression of big-wave tube riding. Teahupo'o's tow days (the place remains a tow-only venue when big) have provided mind-bending spectacle, in the form of logic-defying waves and the risks individuals are willing to take to surf them. On the paddle front, tube-riding at Cloudbreak reached a new peak between 2011 and 2012, when feats on an entirely new level were performed in big, hollow, approachable waves of unsurpassed perfection. Cloudbreak is now the venue where those with the appetite for the biggest paddle tubes in the world hunt, striking whenever the opportunity presents itself.

Quite the contrast is the long coastline of Chile. Wild, cold, and resplendent with powerful waves, Chile has been a region of adventure and discovery over the past decade. Surfers have always been fascinated by the sheer potential of the Chilean coast, which is graced with abundant swell and a multitude of surf setups. As big-wave surfing developed in Chile and the community of big-wave surfers blossomed, a group of talented individuals and new discoveries emerged, rapidly putting big-wave venues on the South Pacific map.

PAGES 128-129: Teahupo'o going subterranean.

THESE PAGES: Believe it or not, Shane Dorian paddled into this wave at a lesser know Tahitian reef he keeps a very close eye on.

CLOUDBREAK

CLOUDBREAK ABRUPTLY COMMENCED a new era over a two-day span in 2011. On July 12 and 13 of that year, a phenomenal swell powered through the Fijian waters and turned Cloudbreak into the place surfing dreams were made of. Surreally large and perfect waves unloaded on this outer reef, blowing the minds of all who witnessed and rode them. The break was surfed by a solid group of the world's best big-wave surfers: Kohl Christensen, Mark Healey, Dave Wassel, Nathan Fletcher, and Bruce Irons led the charge, paddling into some of the most impressive reef-break tubes in the history of the sport. "The conditions were as good as they get," Christensen explains. "I had never seen waves that good. I don't think many people had. We were paddling into some of the biggest, longest barrels ever witnessed."

While Cloudbreak has been prominent in the surf-world consciousness as a perfect offshore reef break since the inception of the Tavarua Island Resort in the '80s, the 2011 swell set the stage for Cloudbreak's future, revealing its potential as a big-wave venue capable of producing the world's best large tubes. Although very rare, days of this size had occurred in the past, but most had gone unridden or undocumented. The 2011 swell marked a paradigm shift.

For the first time in its history as a surf destination, Cloudbreak was open to the public, allowing surfers not staying at the Tavarua Island Resort to chase specific swells by way of a "strike mission." These missions are the mode of operation in the modern big-wave community, and they couldn't go down without open access.

In the three decades preceding this event, the Tavarua Island Resort had exclusive rights to the reef, building the most successful surf resort in the world off the perfection of the waves and the high-quality living at the establishment. It was the Rolls-Royce of surf trips, a total paradise—and if you had the four grand for a weeklong trip, you surfed with only the other guests and employees. Because of the price tag, many surfers never made it to Cloudbreak and large swells were only seen, and at times towed into, by the owners, employees, and guests (whose reservations usually had to be made well in advance). Nothing like what happened in 2011—when a collective group of big-wave surfers were able to "strike" Cloudbreak, based on a specific swell forecast—had occurred during the break's history.

The Fijian government brought this change in policy in 2010, when they declared they would no longer allow private rights to, or ownership of, waves in Fiji. The long-exclusive Tavarua reefs were opened to the public— an overnight game-changer for Fiji's surf and travel scene. Suddenly, anybody could track a swell and surf Cloudbreak. From that moment onward, groundbreaking sessions have gone down each year.

TOP: Tavarua Island

RIGHT: Bruce Irons, one of the best tube riders to ever grace the planet, finding his perfect match at Cloudbreak, July 2011.

Kohl Christensen midway through one of the best rides of all time. "For me everything I'd ever worked for in surfing came together that day, and that wave was a highlight of my life. I had never seen waves that good. I honestly don't think many people had."

THE THUNDERCLOUD SESSION

The July 2011 swell was a game-changer at Cloudbreak. But on June 8, 2012, a swell shook not only the reef but the entire surfing public, producing the best, biggest, hollowest, yet still approachable reef waves ever documented. It's a bold statement, but you'd be pressed to find anyone willing to dispute it. The world's top surfers were there to make the most of it and bring big-wave tube riding to yet another unprecedented level. As Hawaiian Kala Alexander explained, "In my opinion, it was the greatest day of surfing in the history of surfing. I have never seen waves like that in my life."

On June 8, the ASP (Association of Surfing Professionals) World Championship Tour event was in the midst of its waiting period on Tavarua. All the top competitive surfers were there, along with the media. Then along came a giant swell, grabbing the attention of a plethora of big-wave specialists. This legendary gathering set the stage for a historic supersession.

I got to Fiji the day before the swell with a deep crew. The small airport in Nadi, Fiji, was full. Nearly all of the most capable in the business were on site: Twiggy, Ramon Navarro, Kala Alexander, Healey, Greg, Ian Walsh, Kohl Christensen, Jamie Sterling, Kalani Chapman, Peter Mel, Danilo Couto, Billy Kemper, Derek Dunfee, Reef McIntosh, Danny Fuller, Nathan Fletcher, Makua Rothman . . . the list goes on.

The ASP event was already unfolding, and there was a lot of speculation about whether the contest would be held or not. Most of the crew seemed to think they would put the contest on hold, because most of the ASP competitors didn't have the eight-foot-plus boards needed to surf big Cloudbreak, and the prospect of having just two people in the lineup who were mostly ill-equipped didn't seem logical—especially when the swell would drop and give them perfect, more contest-friendly conditions in the days that followed. But who knew? It was a risk everybody took, flying over. The night before, alarms were set to 4:30 a.m. for a 6:00 a.m. departure. Contest or no, we would be out at the reef at first light for a look.

Predawn revealed a torrential downpour, which ended abruptly at dawn with a magnificent bolt of lightning and deep rumbling thunder. The day was powerful from the get-go; it was as if the higher forces of the islands were announcing just that. A big group of us loaded up on the boat Christensen had organized and began the forty-five-minute ride to the reef. The

swell was already there when we pulled into the channel; flawless ten- to twenty-foot waves peeled down the reef.

Not knowing what would happen with the contest, we got right on it. The swell gradually increased over the next two hours as the contest crew made their way to the channel. As the organizers watched, they realized the surf was still manageable, and perfect—and because they liked what was in front of them, the contest was called on. The contest directors cleared the water for the start of competition, right as the first really big sets began breaking on the outer part of the reef. Their call was looking questionable, and most of the competitors began scrambling to borrow boards from us.

ABOVE: Kauai's Danny Fuller, always on point in big left tubes.

LEFT: Stages of preparation to get out to Cloudbreak for the session.

PAGES 138–139: Reef McIntosh: "I had my style of wave I was looking for, and five hours later that wave showed. Straight up wave of my life!"

During the first heat of the day, the swell began filling in, and many of the biggest waves were going unridden. Their size and consistency had magnified. The next heat was the same—so many perfect waves going unridden. By this time, the swell was getting serious, and the ASP surfers were undergunned. Waves of this caliber and quality are a finite resource, and they were going off untouched. It was a painful thing for everybody outside the ASP who'd come to ride them. Everyone knew that was the risk—but it didn't feel right. You can count on one hand the amount of times you may see waves of that quality in a lifetime.

Thankfully, the contest organizers were taking everything into consideration, and they decided to call it off after the second heat and let everybody go surfing. It was a moment of elation for the big-wave crew—and for many of the competitors, including C.J. and Damian Hobgood, Mick Fanning, Joel Parkinson, and John John Florence. Other competitors were visibly nervous and wanted no part of the swell—so very few competitors argued that the event should have kept going. The general consensus was that days like that, being so rare, should not have rules, formats, and regulations.

What ensued was the most incredible tube-riding show of all time. After the contest was called off, the waves got better and bigger, and didn't stop. Most people had never seen anything like what was storming down the reef—even those who had surfed the previous swell in 2011. The conditions conspired to generate upwards of six nonstop hours of twenty- to forty-foot waves with flawless tubes. That wave energy of that magnitude could go so mechanical and approachable was astounding. "I think 2012 had more completed rides than the other big sessions out there, and the talent present was just off the hook," Christensen concludes about the session. "When you put that many talented big-wave surfers together to push each other, something amazing is bound to happen."

LEFT: The ever-comical Dave Wassel, halfway through "throwing a hot dog down a hallway" as he referred to his stellar ride. "After commentating the webcast all day I caught a ride out to the lineup with Slater just in time to see the biggest wave of the day clean out the line up. After that wave Slater put down his board and pulled off his paddle vest, saying, 'That's not what I'm here for.' I replied, 'That's exactly what I'm here for' and dove in. I remember Kai Garcia picking me up on the Jet Ski after my first and only wave and saying, 'You're done. You'll never top that.' Basically I paddled out, caught one wave within minutes, and got kicked out of the lineup by the biggest guy out there."

TEAHUPO'O

TAHITI IS AN EARTHLY PARADISE of the highest order. The dramatic landscape is cosmically vibrant and steeped in beauty, with the greenest of mountains dropping into the bluest of oceans, filled with some of the most remarkable waves this planet can produce. Amid this thriving coral sanctuary of an ocean is Teahupo'o, which, when big, is the thickest, meanest, most astonishingly perfect big-wave slab tube in the world. For some, this wave is a dream and fits perfectly into the surrounding paradise. For most, it's something they would only attempt in their dreams.

The wave lives just off the village of Teahupo'o, for which it is named, where the paved road ends and the landscape turns to impassable mountains. From land, the waves appear like subterranean holes in the ocean. This is because the waves actually drop below sea level, as they feel the contour of the abrupt, extremely shallow reef ledge. Every year, sometime during the months of April through September, Teahupo'o gets legit, and the quiet village sees surfers flood in from around the world in pursuit of these legendary waves.

Towing big Teahupo'o began when Laird Hamilton rode his groundbreaking wave in August of 2001. Nobody had been towed into a wave like Laird's before anywhere in the world—that iconic ride was the beginning— and it spawned a major branch of big-wave

surfing that quickly expanded around the world: giant-tube hunting at shallow, hollow reef slabs, by way of towing in.

The Tahitians, led by Raimana Van Bastolaer, Manoa Drollet, and Vetea David, quickly adapted to towing Teahupo'o. Raimana was there from the get-go. "I witnessed that wave of Laird's. I showed up with my guys and saw the whole thing. It was so gnarly and made us speechless. Mostly when it was that big, we watched. After his ride, he offered me the chance to get a wave, which I tried and got nailed. That day we all realized that wave could be surfed on huge days." It was a revelation that changed Tahitian surfing and opened Teahupo'o up as the biggest tube venue in the world. The bar at Teahupo'o was quickly and dramatically raised, with Raimana, Manoa, and Vetea consistently on the biggest, best waves of every swell, leading the charge, hosting visiting surfers, and getting the wave dialed in.

TOP: For Shane Dorian, "It's pretty hard to beat Polynesia."

OPPOSITE: Koa Rothman, part of the youngest generation of chargers who will shape the future years of big-wave surfing, on one of the thicker waves ridden at Teahupo'o.

PAGES 144–145: Tahitian Manoa Drollet grew up a couple of valleys past Teahupo'o and has an incredible connection with the wave. He's guaranteed to always be on a wave of the day and has ridden a large number of giant tubes with stylish, technical perfection.

CODE RED

It was August 2011. The swell models began predicting waves that sent Teahupo'o-savvy surfers into a paroxysm of excitement, anticipation, and fear. The size, direction, and intensity of the storm predicted left no doubt that the surf would likely be bigger than anyone had seen—and had people asking just how big this freak of nature could get. At Teahupo'o, as with a number of spots only recently pioneered, no one quite knew what was possible.

Adding extra hype to this swell, the ASP and the World Championship Tour were in town for their annual Teahupo'o event. An unprecedented number of good surfers and media were present at ground zero on a giant Teahupo'o day, and the pre-swell froth was churning. On top of that, Teahupo'o's usual suspects—each one a heavy-tube specialist—had begun making their way to Tahiti, sending anticipation into overdrive. The tow-only nature of big Teahupo'o made it likely—much more likely than at Cloudbreak—that the contest would be called off, but having so many people present with a distinct interest in surfing made this an important, uniquely well-documented event.

The projected models never wavered, and the swell arrived with authority, early on August 27. All woke to a violent, frightening ocean. By first light, the size and intensity were historically massive; older Tahitians said they had only seen swell that big in the past twice, well before tow surfing was an option.

"The weather was gray and the whole ocean was moving so much compared to the other big swells. It was really gnarly in the morning. Super west, low tide, and dangerous," was Raimana's early analysis. This wasn't the crystalline-blue perfection of other iconic days. It was raw, furious, and overpowering. The early-morning waves were sketchy, and only a couple people took a chance. Raimana was one of them, and in uncharacteristic form, he ended up with a bad wipeout that sidelined him for the day. That was a sign to wait and let things improve. Raimana nearly always made his waves; his knowledge of the reef was unparalleled. If he'd ended up in a bad situation, it was almost certain that many waves were unmakeable.

As the morning crept on and nerves boiled, the swell began organizing on the reef. Elements melded together that made the waves approachable—even if by the narrowest of margins. It was game on for those who wanted to tow into the biggest, meanest-looking Teahupo'o of all time. Australian heavy-wave

RIGHT: Anthony Walsh

veterans Dylan Longbottom and Laurie Towner, who had teamed up together at Teahupo'o for years, started the show, and made incredible waves right out the gate. That was the cue for others to join the party. Some waves remained unapproachable, twisting into horseshoe shapes and closing down. But others had the right form, and guys with admirable commitment and skill found them—along with the inevitable wipeout. Lots of people went down hard.

Nathan Fletcher, who has a knack for catching the biggest waves of any given swell, rode the wave of the day. Before entering the water, he'd bumped into Kelly Slater and asked him what he thought was going to happen out there. Slater told him somebody was going to get the biggest wave ever at Teahupo'o.

A couple hours later, Nathan found himself deep in the guts of a monstrous fifty-foot-tall tube. He was gobbled by the foam ball before making the wave—but riding as far as he did, through the wave's subterranean innards, was a heroic feat that later earned him the Ride of the Year award.

In May 2013, Teahupo'o did it again, and for several days. This was the closest follow-up to the Code Red day—nearly as big, but with better conditions. As expected, numerous feats

of bravery and dumbfounding rides occurred. But it was the 2011 swell that answered the question of just how big Teahupo'o could get, and revealed what could be the limits of the reef.

OPPOSITE AND ABOVE: What begins as a lump bigger than others as the approach starts on the Jet Ski may just turn into a slab of freakish proportions when dealing with a Code Red type swell. Bruce Irons's shorts were ripped clean off by this beast after it took him down.

TOP: Alex Gray

PAGE 150–151: Nathan Fletcher on one of the largest, heaviest, most technical tube rides of all time.

CHILE

AS THE RECIPIENT OF close-proximity South Pacific swell energy nearly year-round, Chile is one of the most swell-abundant places in the world. The geographic diversity of the country, spanning the forests of the Patagonia region in the south and the bone-dry Atacama Desert in the north, makes Chile a versatile surf destination. Along its 2,700 miles of coastline are waves of all manner—from copious left point breaks to unruly slabs and deep-water outer reefs. Because of the remoteness and inaccessibility of much of the coastline, the region has been ripe for exploration, and significant discoveries continue to be made every winter as big-wave surfing continues to blossom throughout the country.

Big-wave surfing in Chile has gained a global reputation, with Punta de Lobos at the heart of this development. Located in the beautiful, laid-back city of Pichilemu, a three-hour car ride through graceful countryside from Santiago, Lobos is a bustling surf hub that serves as the consistent home break for the local crew, as well as a destination point and base camp for traveling surfers. Waves peel down the long left point break almost every day of the year, and when the close-proximity storms get big enough, Lobos gets large.

Unlike most big-wave spots around the world, Lobos works at all sizes. Most of the time it is a picture-perfect point break, capable of rides lasting more than a minute, but as it gets bigger, the wave breaks farther out, beyond the top of the point, in front of the iconic morros, two rock pinnacles that distinguish this piece of land. Lobos is the ultimate setup for progression into bigger and bigger surf because surfers can literally work up to whatever size they want to hazard, swell by swell, sitting deeper and deeper until they are behind the *morros*, where the risk of getting washed into the rocks is very real. Because of this, big-wave surfing has become a pursuit amongst many who surf along this headland.

TOP: El Buey, in the north, is one of the early big-wave venues in Chile. Ramon Navarro leaning into the tubing left off the reef.

LEFT: The point at Lobos.

ABOVE: The jump-off at the top of the point at Punta Lobos is often the scariest part of the session. Impeccable timing between sets is required as the rocks are unforgiving. Ramon Navarro and crew waiting for the right gap.

On a global scale, Lobos never gets into the extra-large realm, topping out on giant swells at around forty feet. But Lobos is only the beginning in Chile. One local surfer has put Chilean big-wave surfing firmly on the international map, advancing the sport in Chile and spearheading discovery throughout the country. That is Ramon Navarro. Ramon grew up in Pichilemu, the son of a fisherman, and began learning about the ocean from an early age, with Lobos as his home wave. He progressed through the ranks, and by the time he was a young adult, he was the most committed guy on big days, with innate skill. He has Lobos dialed in unlike anybody, and has showcased just how connected he is with this wave during Punta de Lobos's annual Quiksilver

Ceremonial, a big-wave contest that draws the best big-wave surfers in the world.

Ramon is a driven individual with a passion for exploration, and he recognizes just what he has at his fingertips in Chile—several thousand miles of relatively untapped coastline, all of which has the potential for big-wave setups. "The possibilities are huge in Chile, especially in the south where the swells are big, but the weather is an issue. In Chile it's all about timing and new swells—people can find new waves every big swell. It is a really exciting time there, but it is impossible to be in all the places you want to be, because you have so many options and not many big swells each year. It's often hard to make the call." Aside from one other well-known

setup—El Buey, in the far northern town of Arica—no other big waves were being ridden in Chile. But thanks to Ramon, that changed.

Ramon has led an age of exploration and discovery along Chile's coastline, uncovering many large, previously unridden waves. His missions have spanned the frigid waters of the south, the far north, and everywhere in between. He draws in a network of international friends, like Kohl Christensen, Greg Long, and Mark Healey, along with local chargers Diego Medina and Cristian Merello, to make these missions happen. A lot of reconnaissance goes into all these efforts, and not all missions are fruitful, but time after time, new big waves have been discovered.

Santos del Mar is one of the success stories in recent big-wave discovery, although seemingly short-lived. Santos is a deep-water slab, well south of Punta de Lobos, that magnifies swell energy. It's a sketchy wave and nowhere near perfect, but upon finding it and realizing the possibility for really big tubes, Ramon dedicated years to surfing the spot, and rode some amazing waves. The discovery epitomized the fruits of hardy explorations and Ramon's aptitude to ride giant, dangerous, previously unridden waves.

But after a catastrophic 8.8 magnitude earthquake on February 27, 2010, centered near Santos del Mar, the wave changed. The reef had seemingly risen toward the surface after the seismic jolt, making the wave too dangerous to surf. Similar situations have occurred near major seismic areas of Indonesia, as well—stark evidence of wave-riding venues' impermanence in geologically active areas.

Ramon, unfazed, has kept the search going. Since 2010, more discoveries have been made, and the potential of these setups is still being realized. A handful of these new waves are suited for very large paddle-in surfing—unlike Santos, where Jet Ski assistance was required. It is an exciting time in Chile, and the possibilities for groundbreaking events remain very real, and will for many years to come.

THESE PAGES: Ramon Navarro grew up with Punta Lobos (top) as his home break and developed an acute kinship with big waves early on. He has led the charge in Chile this past era, tackling the biggest days, discovering new waves (left), and acting as Chile's international big-wave ambassador, helping to put this pursuit on the map in his beautiful country.

THESE PAGES: Ramon negotiating the imperfections of
Santos del Mar, a discovery he made in Chile's southern
region. "It is a crazy slab, really hard to read. Pretty much
every wave is different and it's almost impossible to see
which one is the perfect one, so you just have to go and try to
get deep from behind the peak."

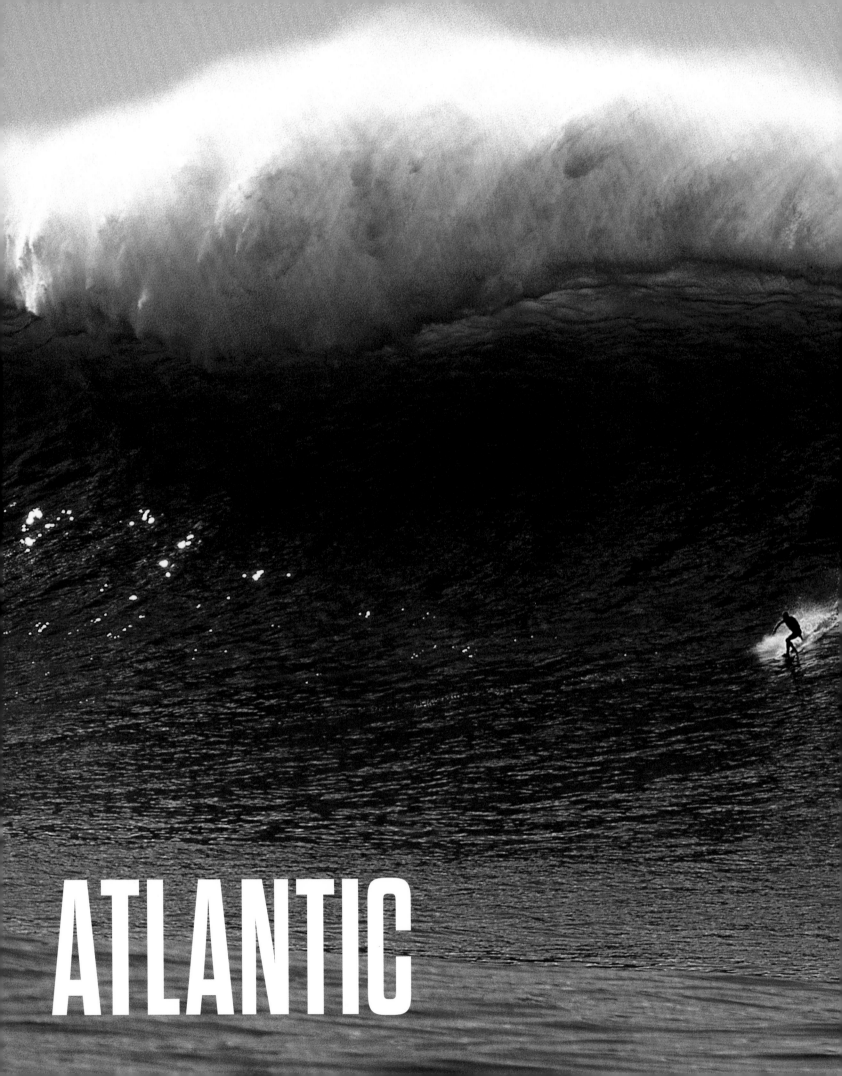

ATLANTIC

The big waves of the Atlantic Ocean are some of the most rugged in the world, loaded with cold, blunt, debilitating power and often detonating among uninviting elements. Two of the ocean's regions—the European waters of the North Atlantic and South Africa in the South Atlantic—are similar in that they are bombarded by giant winter storms that often fail to slack as they move to land. Finding windows of opportunity to ride manageable big waves, and enduring comparatively harsh elements, is seriously challenging in these wild waters, but rewards are very gratifying for the driven individuals who are there when the special moments happen.

The North Atlantic is a raw, ferocious expanse that breeds the largest storms and seas seen anywhere. No other coastlines see actual buoy readings of near forty feet, as the North Atlantic has on recent hallmark swells. There is a unique intensity in storm development and movement here. The compact, extremely cold body of water facilitates massive low pressures, which tend to develop or reach close enough proximity to land to blitzkrieg coasts with gigantic swell. Intense, consistent, incredibly powerful, often unruly, and often enormous waves result. There are giants in these waters, and the abundant wave-riding possibilities have just begun getting tapped, with riveting success.

Big-wave surfing in the region has come leaps and bounds since the turn of the millennium; Europe has morphed into a big-wave region rife with discovery, excitement, and potential. As pioneers explore what's possible on the continent's rugged, stunning coastlines, a few waves have emerged and created worldwide awe.

The awakening and subsequent tackling of Belharra in the Basque region, Nazaré in Portugal, and a plethora of reefs in Ireland have created a small, albeit bustling, big-wave scene in Europe. Before, these waves were left to erupt on their own, watched from a distance by curious surfers. But now, in these three premier locales of the North Atlantic, teams of dedicated individuals and international swell-chasers show up when the rare opportunities to ride in prime conditions arise. And with every swell, the potential of the region becomes clearer and clearer.

The South African waters around Cape Town are a bull's-eye for storms, originating off the notorious Cape Horn, that plow their way through the Roaring Forties (strong west-to-east winds in the Southern Hemisphere) and often slam into the bottom of Africa. Cape Town has a deep surfing heritage, and the big waves of the region are monitored and charged by a devout local crew, who are ready for whatever challenges this precarious piece of ocean delivers. This zone has evolved into an important hub, and the big-wave feats accomplished in these waters are on par with what's happening around the world. Champions, and of the sport are coming from here, using their home to hone their skills as Cape Town, renowned for its dramatically beautiful setting, is one of the Southern Hemisphere's most consistent zones for riding big, challenging waves.

BELHARRA

SINCE THE EARLY 2000s, with the pioneering of Belharra and a number of other reefs, Europe's Basque coast has been unveiling itself to the collective big-wave world as a place of giant surf. Powerful North Atlantic swells have always marched into the Bay of Biscay, but not until the turn of the millennium were big-scale waves like Belharra pursued. Near-shore breaks like Meñakoz and Guéthary helped build a big-wave community in the region, and eventually the insatiable exploratory instincts that are such a large part of surfing eventually led to this unique outer reef.

The Belharra reef lies two miles off the coast of France's Saint-Jean-de-Luz. For years, local surfers peered out with wonder at the reef on the biggest of swells, until it was finally ridden in the winter of 2002–'03—an event that put Europe into the global big-wave mix. Waves well beyond sixty feet were tackled—with Jet Ski assistance—by a local crew that winter led by Sébastien Saint-Jean, Fred Basse, Peyo Lizarazu, and Vincent Lartizien. Belharra revealed itself as a mountainous wave prone to blustery offshore winds, with the Basque countryside as a singular backdrop. This was big news.

As with many outer reefs, Jet Skis and tow surfing were the key components in pioneering Belharra. Since those first sessions, Belharra has come to life every couple of years. A very deep-water setup, which needs the biggest of swells and extreme low tides to break, Belharra produces some of the tallest waves in the world—with waves upwards of seventy feet

ridden and documented—though perhaps not as top to bottom as other waves of this scale.

Images of Belharra are a source of both awe and debate because the wave looks impossibly tall. The spot has generated award-winning rides in the height department at the annual Billabong XXL Awards—most recently in 2011, when French big-wave kingpin Benjamin Sanchis took the Biggest Wave award for his moody, windblown monster. But while giant in height to the point of seeming unreal or photo-graphically deceiving, the wave always has a disclaimer associated with it. Unlike other big-wave locations that see similar face height, like Jaws or Cortes Bank, Belharra doesn't typically break top to bottom—which has led people to downplay its validity. Regardless of where opinions fall, Belharra is a very large wave that takes a tremendous amount of ocean power to break, and the wave carries that power with it. Big waves come in all shapes and forms and Belharra is breathtaking in its unique beauty, and has played a central role in Europe's ascent into the realm of big-wave riding.

PAGES 158–159: Sébastien St. Jean, Belharra.

PAGES 160–161: Greg Long, Dungeons.

TOP: Lookout point at Belharra, which breaks just off the village of St. Jean de Luz, right near the France/Spain border, in the heart of the stunning Basque region.

OPPOSITE: Peyo Lizarazu, part of the local crew who pioneered the wave, tapping into the early morning glory on a day graced with flawless conditions.

LEFT: The speed reached on Belharra's open ocean swells is like few places in the world. French surfer Benjamin Sanchis, who has ridden some of the largest waves at the reef, on the kind of ride that can make the knees shake.

TOP: Benjamin Sanchis

MIDDLE: Peyo Lizarazu

ABOVE: The harbor at St. Jean de Luz.

ANOTHER INEVITABLE . . .

Because of its tall but sloping face, Belharra was thought to offer the opportunity to paddle into a wave well in the "tow" realm more easily than Jaws or Cortes, which present near-vertical wave faces at the takeoff zone. The reef is also surrounded by deep water, causing the wave to back off quickly and ultimately diffuse altogether, minimizing the potential for extended situations of consequence and increasing the capacity for effective rescue efforts. In the light of these unique factors, Belharra seemed to offer the perfect combination for someone to make paddle-surfing history.

In December 2012, Nathan Fletcher, along with Benjamin Sanchis, Dane Gudauskas, and a few of the local crew, made the first attempt at paddling the wave. It wasn't big by Belharra standards—just capping on the reef and backing off quickly—but Fletcher caught a couple of waves and set the stage for future paddle sessions.

The following December, Europe saw one of the most relentless stretches of giant surf on record. Swell after swell battered the continent, and when the requisite elements aligned, Belharra came to life. Once again, there were some very large waves ridden, with Sanchis on the bomb of the day. After reviewing photos from that session, Greg, Twiggy, Dorian, Healey, and a few others decided they could paddle into those waves and set a world record.

The swell train kept on coming, and a storm popped up on the wave models that appeared to take up half the Atlantic Ocean. The center of the storm was creating giant seas—a big gray-and-black blob in the animated swell models. It looked fictitious, unbelievably large, and as days went on, the predicted storm and subsequent swell became a reality. Seas in the center of the storm measured sixty feet, and as it hit the coastline, near-forty-foot seas registered on near-shore buoy readings. The storm was dubbed Hercules, and rarely had so much hype surrounded a swell event anywhere in the world.

Big-wave surfers around the globe took notice; those with the means booked last-minute tickets to Europe. Small crews went their separate ways—some to Ireland to face its moody slabs, others to Morocco in hopes of huge, relatively unknown perfection, and some to Portugal in uneasy anticipation of being the next Nazaré survivor. But it was Twiggy, Dorian, and long-distance paddle champion Jamie Mitchell who made the trip to Belharra, to see if they could test the wave's paddle potential at extreme size alongside Benjamin Sanchis. If there was a crew to make history, this was it.

Given the size of the storm, the possibility of eighty-foot-plus waves was very real. These guys were dead-set on paddling if at all possible, although they did throw a tow board in, too, just in case. On January 6, 2013, Twiggy, Dorian, Mitchell, and Sanchis spent an uneasy day watching and waiting for the swell to arrive. Forecasts predicted the swell would make shore that afternoon, but time passed, the afternoon wore on, and the swell hadn't shown. Right on sunset, it finally hit, and hit quickly, as swells do in Europe. This was not a good thing; the brunt of the energy would pass in the night.

The first fourteen hours (the biggest of the swell) passed unseen, and in the dark broke giants that were likely the biggest waves to hit the reef since its inception as a surf spot. The swell lived up to its name.

The next morning dawned, and as the crew had feared, the brunt of the swell had passed. They were out at first light and took to the expansive, inconsistent, difficult lineup. There were still some very big waves though, one of which cleaned the lineup and broke three boards in the process—but it likely paled next to what would have been breaking through the night.

But there was one distinct highlight of the session. Only a few waves really stood up properly on the reef that morning, and Mitchell was right in the spot for one of them. With a strong offshore wind ripping up the face, he got to his feet on the monster wave. Moments later, the wind and bump on the face launched him off into an avalanche of whitewater. In those few seconds on his feet, another milestone was set: the wave was bigger than anything paddled into before anywhere in the world. Speculation had come to fruition in a valiant, committed effort by Mitchell, who'd seized the rare opportunity to attempt the unknown.

This session, and that wave in particular, opened the door of big-wave surfing possibilities even further.

OPPOSITE: An empty, beautiful monster at Belharra.

JAMIE MITCHELL ON BELHARRA

RL: Paddling into Belharra had only been attempted a couple times before, and on days that were small-scale for this reef. This swell that you, Twiggy, and Dorian were there for was one of the largest anybody has ever seen in any ocean. What were you anticipating, and what was the game plan going into this swell event? Did you have the goal of paddling into the biggest waves of all time?

JAMIE MITCHELL: It was the first time both Twig and I had traveled with a tow board for about four years, so I guess the fact that we packed a tow board meant we thought it might be too big to paddle. I already had two paddleboards in Spain from an earlier trip, and the forecast looked so big that the possibility of it being too big to paddle was real—but we were going there to paddle. That was always the goal, and I guess we got a little lucky that it peaked overnight, because I'm sure there would have been hundred-foot waves during the night.

RL: The wave you caught is probably the biggest wave anybody has ever paddled into. Paddling amongst a new setup is always tricky and comes with an element of trial and error, especially at an expansive outer reef such as Belharra. What was the experience like that day—lining up for a wave, avoiding getting caught inside, and just being out there trying to explore the boundaries of paddle surfing?

JAMIE MITCHELL: It was definitely the hardest lineup I have ever surfed. It felt like you were just sitting in the middle of the ocean, waiting for these huge swells to materialize on the reef. It was hard to even get close to catching a wave. Everyone got cleaned up multiple times. I had been out there for at least two hours before I got that wave. It was like being a goldfish in a swimming pool.

RL: Run us through that ride and the ensuing beating.

JAMIE MITCHELL: I saw the swell a long way out, and Shane Dorian was about thirty yards out from me, so he saw it a touch earlier then me, and I saw him react like something big was coming. When I saw it, I just felt like it was coming straight to me. I had missed so many waves earlier—from paddling out, then swinging—that I thought, "I'm swinging now and just going for it." So I paddled as fast as I could. Twiggy was inside, scratching over it, and he was just screaming at me to go go go go! At that stage, I was so focused on getting up and into a good stance, because the wind was blowing up the face, making it really difficult. I was about ten feet down the face when I stood up, but because the swell was moving so fast and the wind blowing so hard, by the time I got to my feet I was already back up in the lip. At that point, I was just concentrating on keeping my board under control. By the time I hit the third chop, the nose of my board was too high in the air and the wind got under me—and the rest is history. I sort of slid down the face and ended up back to front, then got sucked over with the lip. The violence of the wipeout wasn't crazy bad,

but because I wasn't wearing a leash I got dragged underwater a long way. It felt like I was a fishing lure. By the time I popped up, the next one was pretty close to me, and the whitewater looked like it was connecting with the clouds. It was apparently bigger then the one I had got, and the thing just mowed me and pushed me down pretty deep again, dragging me violently for a long way underwater. I was lucky. The third wave was a small one and just rolled over me, then a ski came and picked me up.

RL: After being amongst the energy of this reef on a large-scale day, how big of a wave do you feel could be paddled successfully at Belharra, given the challenges and elements at hand? Is this where we'll see the tallest waves in this discipline of paddle surfing ridden in the years to come?

JAMIE MITCHELL: I think a wave of the same size can be caught, for sure. Maybe a little bigger. But I think the ocean conditions would have to be so clean—no wind at all—for that to happen. If it's bigger, I'm not sure how much faster the swells would be moving. It was borderline that day, but never say never, right? It's hard to put a size on that day, but it definitely felt like another level as far as ocean conditions—a level I haven't seen or felt before.

THESE PAGES: Jamie Mitchell's valiant effort to paddle into the biggest wave to date, which Twiggy barely scratched over. The next wave of the set was bigger and caught Twiggy inside. It was a radical thirty seconds of life for these two.

IRELAND

THE NORTH ATLANTIC'S frequent, big-scale storms often have high-latitude Ireland in the crosshairs. As a result, big waves batter the coastline almost incessantly, like few places in the world. Until around 2005, big waves off the Irish coast broke in empty lineups. But since then, as big-wave exploration bloomed in Europe and entered Irish waters, setups have been discovered and surfed with regularity by an ever-growing group of Irish and European chargers. Countless setups and options exist along the diverse coastline—many of incredible quality and capable of getting enormous.

Ireland has one of the most dramatic and beautiful coastlines in the world. Verdant pastures lined with ancient, meticulously crafted stone walls lead to the ocean, often with castles looming on distant cliffs and rainbows arching through the sky. Despite the beauty, it's not a place for the faint of heart, in waves of any size, because the far North Atlantic elements are harsh, even on the nice days. Frigid water and air prevail, and are compounded by the hard-hitting ocean. Surfing big waves here takes a special level of dedication and desire.

This craggy coastline has been revealing its charms on the western and northern shores—depending on the direction of a given swell and the local wind conditions—with more breaks than can possibly be surfed by the area's current crew of big-wave seekers. But two waves have been the primary focus of Ireland's big-wave surfing excursions: on the west coast, the setup known as Aileen's, and on the north coast, Mullaghmore Head.

Aileen's lies at the base of the towering Cliffs of Moher. Long have people stood at the edge of the sheer, majestic cliffs and peered the eight hundred feet down to the powerful ocean below. Local surfers Dave Blount and John McCarthy—both with a passion for bigger surf—were aware of a big wave at the bottom of the cliffs long before it was surfed. But just how to approach it was a mystery. This was before Jet Skis, and getting a boat into the ocean on the big days wasn't an option with no nearby harbors open on big days. In 2005, Blount and McCarthy got their first Jet Ski and decided it was time to investigate this wave below the cliffs. An intrepid photographer named Mickey Smith, from Cornwall, England, had come to Ireland with a passion for discovery, and he also helped instigate the early missions to the cliffs. Smith was there to photograph whatever might go down, and he played a key role in pioneering Aileen's.

TOP: Swell lines steaming the bay at Lahinch.

OPPOSITE: Irish surf pioneer Fergal Smith has been instrumental in taking Irish surfing into the heavy water breaks at a world class level. Here Ferg enjoys the golden hour on the Emerald Isle at Aileen's, under the mystical Cliffs of Moher.

Over the course of that winter, the group would launch the ski a few miles up the coast, at a precarious, swell-beaten boat ramp, then motor through wild seas and winds to this remote fragment of earth. The area was rugged, but Aileen's world-class quality became clearer with every passing session, and that kept the passion for chasing the wave fervent. The big, tubing right-hand reef never revealed a flaw, and there seemed to be no size it could not tolerate. The local crew rode great waves every session, and these moments were well documented by Smith, whose images quickly made their way around the world. For Irish surfing, a wave of this scale and quality was big news, and in the years that followed, more and more people began venturing into the lineup.

A goat trail leading down the cliffs became the route in and out as people began paddling from shore. Soon, nearly every good day was ridden. Aileen's quickly became a well-known surf spot, heralded as one of the most breathtaking surfing arenas in the world. Getting locked inside a cavernous tube at Aileen's was just the bonus.

THESE PAGES: Most big wave surfers develop extra special connections with one particular wave. For Tom Lowe, it is Aileen's. "The Cliffs of Moher mean so much to me, not only from a surfing perspective, but also from a deep spiritual sense. The last memory I have of my late best mate Tom Greenaway was at the top of those cliffs, watching the waves together in pure awe. That lasting vision will be with me forever. The wave itself has brought me my biggest highs and most painful lows. I've felt close to death there, dislocated shoulders, broken limbs, and suffered crazy violent hold-downs, which stay with you forever. And through all that I continue to push my personal boundaries out there, growing from each humbling experience, as a surfer and a human being."

MULLAGHMORE HEAD

ON IRELAND'S wave-abundant north coast, near the surfing hub of Bundoran, lies Mullaghmore Head—a beautiful, imposing headland that holds Ireland's most highly documented big wave. Local surfers had long known that big surf broke at the tip of the exposed headland, but the wave's heaviness suppressed the desire to surf it—until Jet Ski assistance became an option. The wave, a roping slab with boils and deformations, really starts working as a big-wave spot at around twenty-five feet. Jet Skis remain necessary when it's big; as with Teahupo'o, the wave's biting ledge is too steep and intense to allow much success when paddling. Navigating the tube also favors a smaller board and the high speed acquired by towing in.

Small days had been ridden at Mullaghmore before big days were hazarded, but when big, the wave became a different animal. Once Jet Skis arrived on the scene, surfers began dissecting this ultra-heavy surf break, playing a major role in the progression of big-wave surfing in Ireland. Since 2005, local and international chargers have annually challenged waves at the top of the intensity scale.

In February 2010, I was privileged to link up with locals Fergal Smith and Tom Lowe, as well as French surfers Benjamin Sanchis and Eric Rebiere. Pulling up at Mullaghmore, we encountered thirty- to forty-foot slabs detonating on the reef, deformed and as sketchy as any lineup I'd seen. For Lowe it was the same. "That was the first time I'd been out to Mully, and it was straight into the deep end! It was freezing cold in the depths of February and the most psycho monstrous waves I'd ever seen!" He was very keen that day though, took the rope first and pulled into a monster right off the bat, showing it was doable and setting the stage. The tide began filling in, making things more approachable as we traded the biggest, coldest, squarest tubes I've ever seen in person. There was never a comfortable moment that session.

In 2013, Kohl Christensen and Danilo Couto flew in from Hawaii for a swell in the upper limit of Mullaghmore's known history. They encountered hailstorms and forty- to sixty-foot monsters. Christensen contends it was the most uncomfortable surfing experience of his life. This is the way it goes at Mullaghmore. Many who've given the place a try—including Twiggy, Greg, Christensen, and Couto—are in no hurry to get back. The local crew, who have adapted to surfing these waters, are the definition of hardcore.

TOP: Mullaghmore in dead of winter is a brutal place to surf. The water is painfully cold, the air is near freezing, and the wind chill is debilitating, which all conspire to make the growling, boil-ridden, extra large slab that much more intimidating.

OPPOSITE: Tom Lowe, in the belly of the beast at Mullaghmore on the harshest of winter days.

LEFT: Between his scores at Mullaghmore and Nazaré, Andrew Cotton has ridden some very large waves.

TOP: Mickey Smith, Fergal Smith, and Tom Lowe.

MIDDLE: Sublime Irish highway.

ABOVE: Coastal Irish cemetary.

STILL OUT THERE . . .

Perhaps the most interesting thing about big-wave surfing in Ireland is its untapped potential. The coast is riddled with sleeping giants—reefs waiting for the right elements to come together. It's not easy to score in Ireland, and it's especially difficult to chance upon an unknown spot during ideal conditions. Intimate knowledge and constant monitoring is key; tide, weather, and swell wait for no one. Spend some time in Ireland and you'll realize surf tends to come in small-window bursts. You have to act fast, and hindsight can be frustratingly clear. Ireland's waves require finicky elements to come together; catching those windows is rare. Then, you have to have the courage to venture out into the biggest seas the ocean can muster, with no safety net beyond the small crew you assemble. The Irish coast is remote, and the country doesn't have big-wave surfing infrastructure like Hawaii or California. It's a step back in time, and to go it here often means going it alone.

Three guys have led the charge at Aileen's and Mullaghmore, and have begun searching out the country's nameless waves. Fergal Smith, Tom Lowe, and photographer Mickey Smith have been on a mission, exploring and pioneering the Irish coast since 2006. When the trio got together, Irish heavy-wave surfing took a big step forward. Lowe comes from Cornwall, as does Mickey, while Fergal is an Irish native. Lowe came to the Irish coast with the right attitude and skill set for surfing the area—determined and always ready. His company elevated Fergal's already insatiable drive. "Lowe turning up changed a lot of things," Mickey explains. "He was entirely unfazed, real talented, and completely committed—to the point of bordering on psychotic—in heavy waves. He was a genuine catalyst for Fergal, because he finally had someone with the same frame of mind and who shared the same visions of possibilities." It was a perfect package: two surfing partners with the same goal, and a dedicated photographer to document it.

No one is more comfortable in Irish waters than Fergal. He comes from Ireland's northwest coast and his years of tireless scouring have likely gained him more knowledge of the temperamental coastlines than anybody. He began venturing into Ireland's powerful waves just as Aileen's came onto the scene, and has since spent unsurpassed amounts of time in heavy-water situations. "Ferg has taken Ireland's surfing so far," says Mickey. "Everything he's achieved is a testament to the lad's ability, imagination, focus, and maturity."

Comprehensively world-class, Fergal has extraordinary drive. I saw his approach firsthand in an area known for its shallow, heavy reefs and small windows of tidal opportunity. He'd bounce from an hour-long session at one spot, stay in his suit, drive fifteen minutes, hit up the next window at another reef until it shut down, eat some food from his packed lunch, drink a cup of tea from his Thermos, put his frigid, wet wetsuit back on in the rain, and get his final session in as darkness fell. Frequently, he surfs on his own, in a climate far from motivational, at spots where you'd generally want a friend or two. He's a perfect, impressive example of a creature adapted to its native environment.

Together, Lowe and Fergal have tested the waters at some of Ireland's unnamed sleeping giants, mammoth waves that every last precaution should be taken with (not unlike approaching giant Cortes Bank). In February 2011, I witnessed the biggest waves I've ever seen while exploring the coast with Fergal and Lowe. The buoy readings were thirty-eight feet at seventeen seconds—unfathomable power. Entering the water that day was life-threatening; having only a small window of time and a bad feeling, we opted out. But similar days await in Irish waters. And as the big-wave world keeps expanding, it's inevitable that someday they will be tested.

THESE PAGES: This was the biggest swell I've ever seen. The near shore buoy was thirty-eight feet, which is nearly unheard of. Seventy-five feet is a conservative assessment of the waves I saw that day. I'd never seen relentless power like that in an ocean, and haven't since.

NAZARÉ

IN LATE JANUARY 2013, the world, and not just the surfing world, was riveted by rumors of a monster wave surfed in Portugal. Headlines in the mainstream media proclaimed that for the first time, the fabled hundred-foot wave may have been ridden at a little-known surf break off the old Portuguese fishing village of Nazaré, by the eccentric, hard-charging Hawaiian surfer Garrett McNamara. And there, alongside the headlines, was a stunning image to back up the claim—one of the most jaw-dropping photos ever taken of a human riding a wave.

This mountain of a wave looked tall beyond belief—a foreboding pyramid of water in a dark, angry-looking sea, McNamara dead center in the mayhem. It made for the biggest big-wave-surfing media sensation ever. Everybody who saw it was awed—including CNN anchor Anderson Cooper, who interviewed McNamara. The interview was composed of hysterical one-liners that nobody in the sport could've come up with besides McNamara. "No rush, so it's probably not one hundred feet," McNamara cackled during his comical summary of the wave.

Getting onto that wave was a testament to McNamara's hard work and determination. He'd set up camp in Nazaré, pursuing the place for more than three years, with the goal of making surfing history—pure and simple—which he fully achieved with that giant wave and iconic image. Was it the hundred-foot wave mainstream media outlets seemed hungry for? Probably not—but it was a giant, and caught at a spot that wasn't on the big-wave map until McNamara went there. Talk about having a vision. McNamara's dedication and instincts for huge surf epitomize the new age of big-wave pioneering. "Garrett has done what we all have wanted to do," Twiggy states. "Find and pioneer a new massive wave—and that is not easy."

The village of Nazaré had always been a sleepy fishing port, moving along at the pace of old-world Europe, until McNamara showed up to surf in 2010. Since then, more and more people have come to witness the ocean's fury. McNamara calls Nazaré "the best place in the entire world to watch and experience giant waves," elaborating, "Nowhere [else] can you safely be as close to all that power." He came prepared to spend the time needed to ride the wave, and he acquired support from the town to create efficient infrastructure.

ABOVE: Nazaré's proximity to shore makes for an intense spectacle.

RIGHT: Shane Dorian taking the paddle approach at Nazaré.

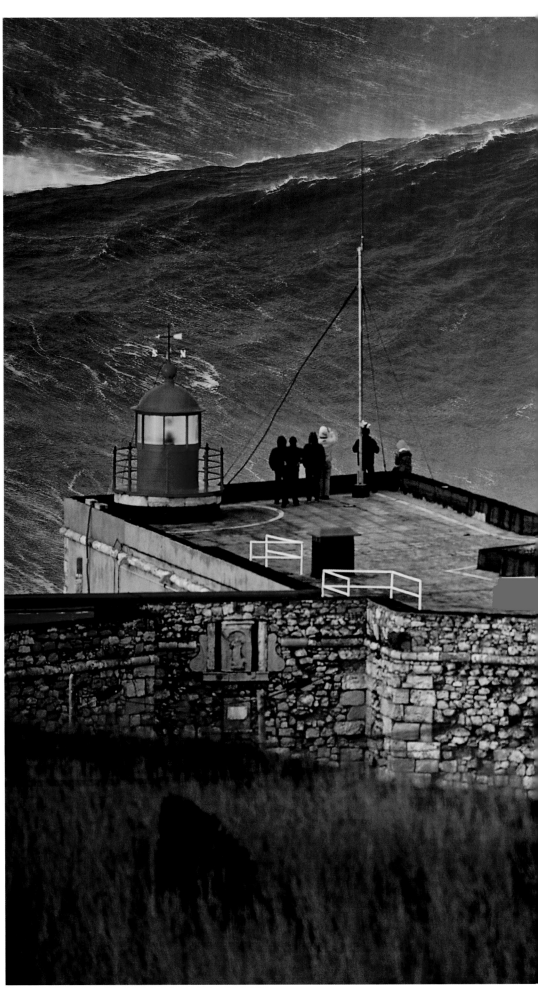

"We had to find good working skis, we had to get insurance, we had to get licenses, we had to have safety on land, and we had to accomplish all of this with no money—just heart, dreams, and an attitude of 'anything is possible,'" explains McNamara. Eventually, ZON—a communications giant in Portugal—offered sponsorship; this helped facilitate the "North Canyon" project, which was purely dedicated to McNamara surfing the wave.

The name "North Canyon" is derived from the bathymetric situation at Nazaré, where deep canyon-like trenches lead right up to land. These canyons carry the full intensity of a swell, concentrating it into ultra-powerful peaks that spike to great heights. At Nazaré, waves stand up and break with seemingly unaccountable irregularity; sometimes they don't break at all, and other times they break top to bottom. It's a peculiar wave in that regard, but there is no disputing Nazaré's power.

Naturally, after McNamara's successful years at Nazaré, more of the big-wave community grew interested. The winter following McNamara's giant wave, Brazilian big-wave veteran Carlos Burle set up camp in Nazaré with his tow-surfing partner Maya Gabeira, one of the world's most accomplished female big-wave surfers. Portugal was an easy place for the Brazilians to acclimate, and like McNamara, they settled into the community and waited for the North Atlantic to funnel some giant peaks down the underwater canyons.

ABOVE: Garrett McNamara in his workshop.

RIGHT: Garrett McNamara and the wave that went around the world as the "one-hundred-footer." Is it that? No. Giant? Yes, and with unfathomable amounts of power.

ABOVE: Carlos Burle on a Nazaré mountain, October 2013. This was his only ride of the day upon going back out after Maya's incident. He made it count, in the calculated "one and done" kind of way.

On October 28, 2013, the day they'd been waiting, training, and hoping for came. Peaks of a similar size to McNamara's were standing up, shifting, wedging, and breaking, in the strange way they do. Unfavorable wind was predicted to come up quickly, so the crew was on it at first light.

Gabeira was up first. Just as the sun hit the water, a giant set peaked on the horizon. Knowing the conditions were forecast to deteriorate and the opportunity for a good wave was slim, Gabeira committed to the biggest wave of her life. Unlike many waves that don't fully break at Nazaré, this one did—and it

the second I lost my vest from the impact while still under water. When I came up I was in pretty bad shape," Maya recounts. It was the beating of a lifetime, and that first hold-down was just the beginning. She was subsequently beaten by the waves that followed, until the point of near blackout. Burle was able to get to her, and she grabbed hold of the towrope in a last effort to get pulled away from the impact zone. She made it a small distance; then her body shut down. She blacked out.

Fortunately, they were near shore at this point, and Burle was able to retrieve her and drag her up the beach, where CPR was administered. After a couple minutes, she regained consciousness. It was a close call, but they did everything they had trained to do, and her life was saved.

One would think that after such an event Burle would be done for the day, but he wanted a wave. After Gabeira had been taken to the hospital, he got back out there with a serious set of mental armor on, and made it count. His first and only wave of the day, he wrangled a giant. It was an emotional day at this one-of-a-kind break that plays a fascinating role in the ongoing process of taking big-wave surfing further, and pushing the sport to unimagined new levels.

ABOVE AND BELOW: Brazilian Maya Gabeira has racked up a lot of miles chasing big waves this past decade in extremely devout fashion with her tow partner Carlos Burle. This is the biggest wave a female surfer has ridden. Ultimately it almost cost Maya her life.

carried all the weight of its size. Gabeira flew down the face of the wave, hitting bump after bump, trying to maintain. "I just focused on trying to manage the bumps, but on the third one I lost control and the next thing I knew I was on my back with the wave unfolding on top of me. That kept me under for two waves and on

LEFT: The ultra stylish Hawaiian
Kealii Mamala, November 2014.

CAPE TOWN IS NOT an inviting place for a big-wave surfer. Some of the most treacherous seas in the world batter the area, generated by storms that power across the notorious Roaring Forties latitude line, carrying cold Antarctic air with them. These frigid fronts make for giant waves, and through the winter there is usually no shortage of intimidating surf. Finding windows that are manageable is tricky; oftentimes, Cape Town is plagued by "victory at sea" conditions, which send surfers up the coast seeking more sheltered areas.

Cape Town is blessed with two predominant big-wave setups, Dungeons and Sunset. Together they've bred a contingent of world-class big-wave surfers: Twiggy, Chris Bertish, and Andrew Marr all cut their teeth at these rogue surf spots, making the world's other lineups seem almost friendly in comparison. "This is like Disneyland," Bertish remarked about Isla Todos Santos on his first day there, in forty- to fifty-foot surf. After visiting Cape Town, a few years after hearing that remark, I understood his thinking.

Both waves lurk at the promontory points on either side of the expansive Hout Bay, about five miles from each other. The deep bay draws in the full brunt of swell, focusing it on both Sunset and Dungeons. These waves are close in proximity, but they differ drastically, and work in different wind conditions—a major bonus for big-wave surfers in Cape Town.

Dungeons is an ominous big-wave lineup to paddle. Many places in the world have a distinct lineup and somewhat predictable movement to the waves; Dungeons does not. The lineup stretches over more than a hundred yards, and waves break all over its vast playing field. In prime form, it's a world-class big wave, showing its stripes every couple of years. Cleanups are common, and the surroundings, while stunning, impart a sense of perilous exposure—similar to how one would feel roaming a remote region full of lions. Part of this is because of the great white sharks.

The reef lies in front of the iconic Sentinel cliff, a spire of land at the mouth of Hout Bay. Below the base of the Sentinel is a deep-water channel about five hundred yards wide, separating the land from where the waves finally dissipate. As long as people have been surfing here, this section of turbulent, deep water has been known as Shark Alley. A seal colony lives at the far northern part of this channel, and the prolific great white sharks of the area have been known to frequent that area for food, cruising the channel to get there. This extra element of danger alerts every sense in your body. When mortality threatens from all angles, you feel that much more alive, and Dungeons is sensory overload.

LEFT: Frank Solomon, Dungeons.

ABOVE: The "Shark Alley" inside of Dungeons.

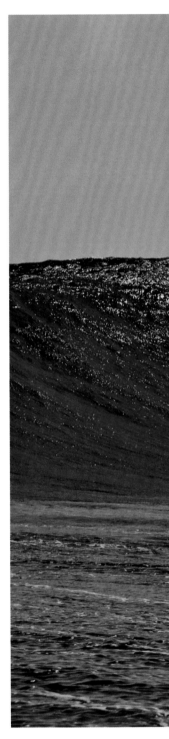

ABOVE: Chris Bertish, Sunset.

BELOW: The wild, unruly ocean of Cape Town.

OPPOSITE: Twiggy, Dungeons.

The wave was pioneered by a hardcore group of locals who braved the giant waves and sharky waters, paddling from land without the addition of any modern lifesaving tools, or even boats. They would paddle out and paddle in—or sometimes swim in, if a leash or board broke. This was charging at its most primal; ultimately it set the future for a more organized approach to the wave.

The Dungeons surfing approach evolved and escalated with the first contest—the Big Wave Africa, put on by Red Bull in 2000. Proper thirty- to forty-foot surf graced that first event, which South Africa's Sean Holmes won. Suddenly Dungeons was beamed onto the international scene. In the years that followed, Red Bull continued to market this wave through the event, and began drawing in a mixed international and national group, where the surfers spent a month in Cape Town each winter for the contest waiting period.

These years made for legendary gatherings, a couple of which I was there for. Most competitors were housed together in a sprawling compound in the upscale Hout Bay part of town, right by Dungeons. Many friendships were born, and the collective group environment bred progression in the lineup and wild times on land. Every opportunity to surf the reef during this time was seized; when that many good surfers are together, things advance, people go for it. Greg won the event in 2003, the second time it ran; it was his first major contest win, and it propelled him onto his current path as the most decorated big-wave surfer in the world.

More international surfers began taking interest in Dungeons; at the same time, the local crew was growing and getting the wave dialed, creating an exciting era of wave riding at Dungeons.

The beautiful thing about big-wave surfing in Cape Town is that when Dungeons isn't working, Sunset often is. It's a remarkably different wave, world-class and treasured by the Cape Town crew. The near-perfect reef is shapely and consistent, focusing in nearly the same spot every time—unlike its counterpart in Dungeons. The powerful bowling right predominates, bending back on itself, actually gaining momentum along the reef. Immaculate perfection

occurs more regularly here because of the reef's perfect shape and the offshore southeast wind, which acts as an efficient grooming agent. Sunset hasn't received the international limelight that Dungeons has, leaving its share of incredible days to the hardy local Cape Town chargers— Andrew Marr, Simon Lowe, Micky Duffus, Ian Armstrong, and many others. These locals have dedicated countless hours to riding Sunset, and have developed into outstanding big-wave riders in the process.

The most accomplished big-wave rider to come from this part of the world is Grant "Twiggy" Baker. He's been there for most of the hallmark days in Cape Town. While his hometown is Durban, in the warmer climes of the country, he has dedicated himself to surfing the Cape Town winters; Dungeons and Sunset have been a major factor in his development as one of the best big-wave surfers of all time. Anytime Twiggy surfs, he is on at least one of the best waves of the day. His prowess at all the historic sessions he has been a part of, competitions included, is at the absolute upper echelon of the sport. He rarely makes mistakes, and constantly blows minds, which has made the name "Twiggy" synonymous with the best of what happens in our sport. "Cape Town," he explains, "has made me the big-wave surfer that I am."

ABOVE: Twiggy, first descent at Tafelberg Reef, outside of Dungeons. For many years Twiggy speculated the biggest wave in Africa could be ridden there. Chances to surf the reef are rare so when a fleeting moment appeared, Twig and Greg pounced. "I actually don't remember Greg even having to chase this wave down, it was almost as if the swell had picked us out from two thousand kilometers away. Greg towed me in perfectly, and right then was when the luck went out the window. The wave was moving at twice the speed I had ever felt and even though the first wave had done some cleaning, it was still ridiculously bumpy, and I was picking up speed at a rate of knots! Before I knew it, I was completely out of control, barely hanging in the straps with my toes and only able to go in a straight line, skipping down the face doing multiple jumps over these moguls in the face. The wave felt huge when I finally got to the bottom but I still couldn't turn, and just managed to outrun the lip before getting mowed by the foam."

ABOVE RIGHT AND RIGHT: There is a very competent crew in Cape Town who keep the lineups of Dungeons and Sunset at a high level, always prepared for any day that comes their way. These two want the bombs: Matt Bromley (right), and Mike Schelback (top right).

THESE PAGES: Cape Town local and underground legend Andrew Marr lived directly in front of Sunset for many years and has a deep bond with the wave. His highly attuned surfing and gregarious character have been the source of inspiration for all who have come in contact with him throughout his years chasing big waves in South Africa and Oahu's North Shore, his other seasonal home for more than a decade. For Twiggy, he has been a very important figure in South African big-wave surfing: "Mr. Marr is a legend in the Cape Town surf scene and to me is the best big-wave rider out of South Africa over the past ten years. He is an inspiration to many, and the only difference between us is that he doesn't like to compete, but on any given day at Sunset or Dungeons he out-surfs me every time with meticulous positioning and a wave knowledge that indicates a lifelong dedication to existing in a wild ocean.

"On top of this he is one of the funniest, down-to-earth people you will ever meet and has, along with Mickey Duffus, paved the way for many a South African surfer heading to Oahu. To this day, every time that I surf the North Shore someone asks me how he is doing and to send their love—and this is after three years of absence from the area. If that isn't testament to a good character I don't know what is."

AUSTRAL
WATERS

In the underbelly of the Australian continent, from Southwest Australia over to Tasmania, a distinct region is renowned for the development of hardcore big-wave "slab" surfing. While West Oz (Western Australia) is part of the Indian Ocean, and Tasmania part of the Tasman Sea, as a generalization—to keep this zone classified together because of the same feel, vibe, and big-wave movement—I'm referring to the overall region as the Austral Waters.

The collective regions are beneficiaries of the brutally intense storms that scuttle up off Antarctica and then along the Roaring Forties during the Southern Hemisphere's winter months. Some swells come with the weather; others are clean and crisp, imploding on the plentiful abrupt reef shelves and manifesting as slabbing tubes (many of which remain questionably surfable). No other region boasts such a high quantity of radical big-wave tubes: Cow Bombie and the Right in West Oz, Shipsterns and Pedra Branca in Tasmania. And the local population of surfers is hell-bent on riding them.

Tow surfing made approaching the waves possible and Australians, being the no-frills, no-worries, up-for-anything mad dogs they are, have tackled their ferocious slabs with a no-holds-barred approach, writing a new chapter in the book of big-wave surfing. The country's deep surfing heritage and thriving surf population have resulted in an abundance of skilled surfers, keen on one-upping their mates.

Possibilities and consequences have been well documented throughout the Austral Waters, and continue to awe the collective surf world. These waves are just the beginning, too. Remote but explorable territory and more technical missions are waiting. And one thing is for sure: when a group of hardcore Aussies come across something heavy—remote and dangerous though it may be—they are going to go, and go hard.

PAGES 196–197: Tyler Hollmer-Cross, Shipsterns.

LEFT: Paul Morgan, paddle perfection at Cow Bombie.

COW BOMBIE

AUSTRALIA'S SOUTHWEST corner has long been a haven for surfers with a penchant for powerful waves. It's an amazing part of the world. The pace is slow, and the quality of life is superb. Old-growth eucalyptus forests and vineyards blanket rolling hills that lead to a clean, swell-abundant ocean. The region, with the village of Margaret River at its heart, has often drawn comparisons to Oahu's North Shore, for the numerous powerful setups within relatively close proximity. And like the North Shore, all these powerful waves have bred one of the most solid groups of surfers condensed in any one part of the world.

For about eight months of the year, the southwest corner is a catcher's mitt for near-unrivaled amounts of swell. It's on the same Roaring Forties track as South Africa and often the same storms that pass the African continent steam through the Indian Ocean and blast swell into West Oz. While at times the area endures long periods of foul weather, it also consistently receives ultra-clean, pristine swells, bringing the region's biggest waves to life.

Despite its long history as a surfing region, West Oz remains a prime location for discovery. What has been uncovered in this area is mighty impressive. A couple absolute dinosaurs of waves have come onto the scene, and hard-charging Aussie madmen have pioneered them with gusto, to the delight of the surf-stoked continent.

Two breaks in particular, Cow Bombie and the Right, have been the most significant recent discoveries. They are drastically different waves. Cow is a deep-water, open-ocean setup, with similarities to Jaws or Cortes. The Right is a mutant slab. Each has drawn a different audience, though there's some crossover between the two. Both, though, require the utmost commitment.

Cow Bombie is located off the small village of Gracetown, home of the famous North Point break, a crown jewel of West Oz surfing. People used to see distant explosions of whitewater on the horizon, several miles out to sea, as swells detonated on an unexplored reef. This was Cow Bombie. And when a couple Jet Skis finally got in the mix, recon of this outer-water mysto wave began. Local chargers Damon Eastaugh, Paul "Antman" Paterson, Damien "Taco" Warr, and a few others revealed the reef's extra-large, high-quality potential in early missions, and anticipation grew in the local big-wave community. The spot had a unique dynamic capable of turning deep ocean swells into giant waves, much like Cortes Bank. But unlike Cortes, this piece of reef is relatively small, focusing sea energy into a condensed peak, forcing it to break top to bottom.

Each mission led to more speculation and higher hopes. Big waves were ridden during early sessions, but nothing in the extra-large realm. But the crew persisted—and on July 5, 2006, flawless fifty- to sixty-foot waves unloaded on the reef, looking as good and majestic as anywhere. Antman, one of the best big-wave surfers in the world at the time was waiting for this day. "That session really set the bar for what Cow Bombie was capable of and how crazy some of the mad dogs that surfed it are.

"Damon and I were the first out in the dark and I'll never forget when we arrived at the bombie. The volume of water, the power, and the speed, were next level for us. We looked at

ABOVE: The Gracetown carpark, launching point for Cow Bombie.

RIGHT: Damon Eastaugh is a local winemaker and pioneer at Cow Bombie. Partnered with Paul "Antman" Paterson, this was the session they realized just what they had in their neighborhood, July 5, 2006.

LEFT: West Oz has one of the most solid groups of surfers in the world, bred by the abundance of powerful, critical waves. Damien "Taco" Warr is a low-key charger very attuned to the region—the kind of guy who's always in the right place at the right time.

each other, and Damon threw me the rope. The first wave was a small, warm-up wave, but the second was probably the biggest wave I've ridden in my life. As more crew hit the bombie, Damon and I were a little more selective using our turn wisely, resulting in Damon riding one of the biggest waves we'll ever see in West Oz." That day put this little-known reef firmly on the map for big-wave hunters.

The drive to paddle Cow eventually grew—but the challenge of paddling a place as far out to sea as Cow is enormous, because there are no landmarks to line up with, and the danger of being caught inside is compounded by this fact. There is a very real feeling of being adrift at sea at places like this, which makes it extremely hard to be in the right spot.

A few less-than-impressive days were sampled by means of paddling as preparation. The perfect day would come, and a handful of surfers would make the most of it. In mid-October 2011, everything came together. Hard-charging paddle champion Jamie Mitchell flew over from his home on the Gold Coast. Paul Morgan, a quiet southeast coast charger who had paddled Cow before, was ready. And the local eccentric surfboard developer and vagabond traveler known as Camel, who had recently become obsessed with paddling the biggest Australian waves he could find, rounded out the trio who really went hard that day. They banded together in the tricky lineup and paddled into the biggest waves to date at the reef.

The swell was a perfect size, hovering around thirty- to forty-foot faces, and the conditions were pristine, with light offshore wind and beaming sunshine. It was as good a day as possible for paddle-surfing the reef, one of those days that will always be a point of reference. As of 2015, such good conditions haven't coincided with another opportunity. As with many big-wave spots, Cow may have years of slumber or unfavorable conditions before the rare perfect day comes again.

Jamie Mitchell has kept his perspective and knows just how fortunate they were. "That day at Cow Bombie was special," he says. "We had surfed it the afternoon before, and it was raw and windy and pretty ugly. The next day when we woke, it was just so clean and beautiful with a slight offshore wind. When we paddled out, the wind basically backed off to dead winds and the tide got super low. For the swell, wind, and low tide to come together for that one day is pretty amazing—that it went down in raw Western Australia, and two miles out to sea, makes it very rare!"

RIGHT: Camel is a fixture of West Oz surfing, known for living in his van near good waves in the region and getting highly connected with them. In recent years, he's focused his energy into paddling the biggest waves he can find and has ridden some absolute beauties.

THESE PAGES: Jamie Mitchell, very
content after a session like this.

206   THE FINEST LINE

THE RIGHT

THE RIGHT is an entirely different specimen of wave—a monstrous, mutant slab. The reef is composed of an underwater pinnacle that pops up and very abruptly drops off, and when deep, powerful groundswells hit the point, the ocean folds over itself with the highest-magnitude power, thickness, and intensity. The wave is hectic to surf; many who've ridden it have experienced scary situations that make them question their motives. To top it off, the south coast of Western Australia remains a true wilderness, teeming with one of the most abundant great white shark populations in the world, something that's hard to get off the mind. Help is a long way away if anything goes wrong, making the region one of the world's most dangerous surfing zones.

A gnarly breed of slab hunter has taken to the Right. The wave is similar to its Tasmanian counterpart, Shipsterns; no one knows what will ensue when the towrope is tossed and the ride begins. Some waves are makeable, producing a cartoonish tube that seems to cheat physics. Others warp down on themselves, creating impossible situations, at a size and power rarely duplicated.

Wipeouts have led to very similar near-death experiences for three of the best at this type of surfing: Antman, Mark Mathews, and Ryan Hipwood. All were shoved down to extreme depths just off the backside of the reef, enduring both a massive struggle against the currents to get back to the top, as well as extremely long, multiple-wave hold-downs. It's a high-risk, high-reward wave. For Antman, it was the scariest situation he's encountered. "The wave looked fine but when the clamp appeared I was at the point of no return and knew a

TOP LEFT: Twiggy

ABOVE: Paul "Antman" Paterson is the epitome of the gnarly West Oz breed of chargers who are typically unfazed by much. He got caught in a no-win situation here that made for the wipeout of his life, plunging him into the lonely depths the Right is notorious for.

destructive pounding was inevitable! It took me off the edge of the reef, down into the abyss and tumbled me violently, taking me deeper and deeper. Just when I thought I'd had a beating of a lifetime and was heading for the surface, the second wave passed over, sending me back into a tumble. I went into survival mode and really relaxed and eventually surfaced on the third

wave that backed off and didn't break. Twig got to me and then we had to scramble out of the zone as the fourth wave was another twenty-foot chunk of ocean. I still don't think my inner ear and head have been the same since that day. The pressure on your head is so intense after being pushed that deep.'' Entering the water there means facing this potential reality.

THESE PAGES: Chris Ross (above), Laurie Towner (opposite top), and Ryan Hipwood (opposite bottom) are three of Australia's most highly skilled slab hunters.

MARK MATHEWS ON THE RIGHT

RL: The Right is one of the thickest waves in the world, with a fair amount of unpredictability about it. What's the feeling of surfing out there on a big day, knowing that you are looking for the biggest slab you can find, and not knowing quite what you may be in for when you let go of the rope?

MARK MATHEWS: For me, it is the best feeling in surfing. Everything about the place is so raw and powerful. There is this moment when you first pull into a barrel, and the full force of the ocean folds over you—it's like a river of water draining off the reef, trying to suck you up the face and into the lip. You're digging your toes in, doing everything not to fall. Then you get to a point inside the barrel where you have done everything right, you're in the perfect position, and for the next two or three seconds you get to stand back in complete awe of what's going on around you. There is no feeling in surfing as amazing as those two or three seconds. I've heard of astronauts being completely taken back by earth's beauty when they look at it from on the moon. I figure that two or three seconds standing in the barrel at the Right is like going to the moon.

RL: How difficult of a wave is it to ride and judge?

MARK MATHEWS: It is super tricky to position yourself deep in the barrel out there. The wave sucks so hard off the reef that it seems to stand still for a moment before it breaks. You come in with so much speed from the ski that you have to put yourself in a position where it looks like there is no way you can make it. It's a really scary thing to do. It goes against all your natural survival instincts.

RL: A number of you guys who surf the place the hardest have encountered some pretty harrowing wipeout situations. What was your personal experience like?

MARK MATHEWS: I think it would be like falling off an underwater version of Niagara Falls. You go through this crazy weightless feeling as the wave sucks, then it's like a massive explosion going off as it drives you into the deep black abyss. There is so much pressure down there, it feels like your head is going to explode. Then, when it finally lets you go, you start the long swim up to the surface, just praying another one won't break on you before you get up.

TASMANIA

IT IS FITTING for this insanely rugged surf spot to exist at the bottom of the world in southern Tasmania—a place so remote, raw, and at the full mercy of the elements a wave this wild just had to be on its shores. Shipstern Bluff (aka Shipsterns, or Shippies) is the patriarch of a type of hardcore slab surfing that developed after the new millennium, in Australian waters especially. Places once deemed unrideable have been systematically pioneered. This wave has proved what is possible—and oftentimes what's not.

Not much is friendly or inviting about the place when a massive Roaring Forties–generated swell pounds the reef. The water is cold, the air is icy, and breaking right in front of a massive cliff is Shippies, a mutant riddled with ugly deformities in the form of boils, steps, and ledges. But once past these imperfections, one of the world's biggest, most impressive tubes comes together, and slab-hunting chargers eagerly tackle it.

Shipsterns entered the spotlight in 2001, after a mission in which two of Australia's best slab surfers, Mark Mathews and Kieren Perrow,

hiked a two-mile trail through thick Tasmanian forest, the only route in by land, and scored the wave. Both of these guys are incredibly gifted, and the pictures that circled the world from their first voyage were stunning. Mathews and Perrow rode incredible, ultra-heavy waves, masterfully negotiating the steps and locking into some big tubes. That trip expanded the surfing world; Shipsterns was the most outrageous slabbing wave ridden at that point in time.

Before that, only a local surfer named Andy Campbell had walked that same trail down, surfing out there by himself for years—a ballsy endeavor. After 2001, that all changed. A solid crew of Tasmanian surfers began riding the wave; the best Australian chargers began making the short flight down; and the beastly slab went on to play a major role in the high-risk, high-reward slab-surfing world.

Shippies can be paddled, up to a point, but the Ski is necessary on big days. Then, Shipsterns's deformities, tubes, and risks unfold on a grand scale. Any time somebody lets go of the towrope on a big-set wave, they roll the dice: Many waves are simply unmakeable. Out there it's blind courage, with an emphasis on courage. Injuries have been frequent and severe. Mark Mathews broke his back after a bad wipeout, and nearly every frequent rider has a survival story.

TOP: Overlook at Shipsterns.

OPPOSITE: Mikey Brennan, Shipsterns.

ABOVE: The mutant steps that define Shipstern Bluff. Letting go of the tow rope on a wave this size is a complete roll of the dice. Ryan Hipwood is poised for a perfect landing directly into another predicament of seriously uneven water.

OPPOSITE: The bluff for which Shipsterns got its name. Getting washed into it is a reality.

But the Shipsterns coin also has a shiny side. Occasionally, depending on swell direction and tide, the boils and ledges don't affect the waves severely, or are at least navigable. On these days, the reef produces some of the world's largest tubes.

Over the past decade, the wave has bred a generation of Tasmanian surfers who are incredibly enthusiastic, albeit a bit nutty. Marti Paradisis, Mikey Brennan, James and Tyler Hollmer-Cross, and a handful of others have gotten to know Shipsterns in and out. This no-frills group takes pleasure in all aspects of surfing here—radical wipeouts included. They collectively tackle big sessions like a team, looking for the biggest, freakiest waves of the day—"stoinkers," as they call them. A stoinker can be a giant tube ride, or just an unmakeable

mutant and they are what these guys want. It is charging at its most essential. No hesitation. Slightly psychotic.

Usually a base-camp boat hovers around the channel; it's owned by a humorous guy named Pauly, and it's always packed to the brim with the crew as they take turns surfing. From the sidelines, the crew cheers and screams as Pauly honks the boat horn, calling their friends into the radical waves. It's a mad little surfing group. Regardless of the outcome, the cheers continue, and keep going all day as the surfers cycle around. Such is the state of slab surfing in Tasmania.

Tasmania has significant swell activity and untapped coastline, and this dedicated crew knew there had to be more setups in the area. What came next in Tasmania was Pedra Branca,

a wave that upped the stakes even further. The setup lies sixteen miles out to sea directly off the southern tip of the island, at a reef just off a series of pinnacle rock outcroppings notorious as a great white hangout. Pedra's deep, open ocean power, combined with its shallow reef, make it extremely perilous—an intimidating mix between Cortes Bank and Shipsterns.

On the first mission to Pedra Branca, the local crew, along with Ross Clarke-Jones and Tom Carroll, scored what remains the best day yet. They've been on it nearly every chance since, riding the biggest waves of their lives, taking the most intense beatings of their lives, and chalking it all up to adventure. They are always ready for the next opportunity to get back to this eerie piece of the ocean and see just what Pedra is capable of.

"IT IS CHARGING AT ITS MOST ESSENTIAL. NO HESITATION. SLIGHTLY PSYCHOTIC."

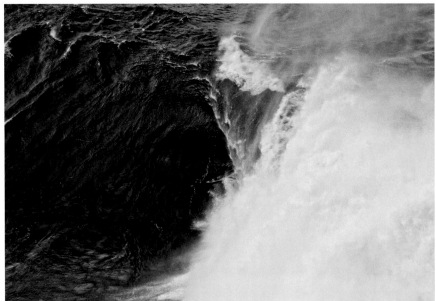

LEFT, TOP: James Hollmer-Cross, Shipsterns.

LEFT, MIDDLE: Rudi Schwartz, Shipsterns.

LEFT, BOTTOM: Mark Mathews, Shipsterns.

ABOVE: Mikey Brennan saluting the "Stern." His catlike reflexes on this wave are truly remarkable.

THESE PAGES: The Hollmer-Cross brothers (above), James (left) and Tyler, went blow-for-blow this session on two of the biggest Pedra waves ever ridden, which both ended in harrowing wipeouts. They are incredibly comfortable and capable in their home waters.

THESE PAGES: Legends of the sport, Ross Clarke-Jones and tow partner Tom Carroll teamed up with the Tassie crew on the first expedition to surf Pedra. The conditions were flawless and everybody was blown away by what existed at this outer water reef, sixteen miles off the southern tip of Tasmania. There is an element of trial and error any time a new big wave is surfed, especially in rugged outer waters. Ross was stuck with no other option than to literally get blown away when this wave shifted and grew down the line. "He did the perfect thing ejecting off the back and not running into the lip," according to Carroll. "He came up completely cross-eyed from that one though, way far away from the break. We didn't know what we were in for out there."

MARTI PARADISIS ON TASMANIA

Tasmanian native Marti Paradisis has been at the leading edge of this generation's heavy-water scene, helping expand the boundaries at Shipsterns and Pedra. He's a humble, driven individual and a gifted surfer; time and again, riding astonishing waves. He's spent as much time in Tasmania's lineups as anybody, and knows just what is at stake.

RL: You guys have a classic, hard-charging scene down there. What's the vibe like on a big day?

MARTI PARADISIS: We're a pretty close team. Generally we hang together, chase swells together, and we all want to be a part of it. The worst is missing a good session. Usually before a big swell, we all touch base over the phone and suss out a plan. If it's at Shippies, you know everyone will meet at the boat ramp at first light. But for bigger adventures, it takes a day or so to organize the logistics. All the boys are on the same program mentally, and we know we can count on each other if the shit hits the fan.

RL: Surfing Shipsterns looks very technical when it's big. It seems you and other locals, like Mikey Brennan and the Hollmer-Cross brothers, are really comfortable and tuned into the wave. Does that just come with time spent riding it?

MARTI PARADISIS: Time and experience out there is essential. To be able to recognize which part of the reef the wave is focusing on, and knowing what the wave does when it hits each section, is what determines which line you take on the wave. When it's big, it goes into another level. Your experience becomes second nature, and ultimately the wave will have the final say. Once you're into one of those beasts all the elements come into play, but sometimes it's just plain luck that will get you through.

ABOVE AND OPPOSITE: Marti Paradisis, Pedra.

PAGES 226–227: Ross Clarke-Jones, Pedra.

RL: Is it still a constant challenge?

MARTI PARADISIS: Shippies is always a challenge. There's always a level to be pushed out there and always will be. Because of its unpredictability, to be able to get the place completely wired seems impossible. But you do get days when you feel you have it covered—then a step will pop up outta nowhere, you faceplant, and reality sets in.

But the big low-tide days are crazy. As you let go of the rope you can already see the way the wave is molding itself around the reef. There's certain things you look for to see what the wave might do, like how shallow it looks, the angle of the swell, whether it's doubling up, et cetera. If it's a big swell line approaching, it definitely tingles the nerves, and the excitement is overwhelming.

RL: Seems like everybody has had to take some bad wipeouts over the years. What is your worst, and what is the worst you have witnessed?

MARTI PARADISIS: My worst wipeout at Shippies was caused by a wave that wasn't very big, but it rolled me straight through the rocks. While I was underwater I hit the rocks; this was quite normal, so I didn't think anything of it. All of a sudden, my leg rope snagged and I stopped. With the force of the turbulence pulling me one way, I couldn't physically reach the leash to unhitch myself. I knew I was right near the surface, but I still wasn't able to quite get a breath. I tried a few more times to no avail, each time using valuable energy. Then the second wave hit. I just had to try to remain calm. As I was losing oxygen, I started to lose concentration. Then something clicked, and I snapped out of it, realizing the turbulence had subsided. I used the last of my energy and lunged at my leg rope, luckily getting it on the first go. As I popped up, Andy Campbell was there on the ski. I laid on the sled for about five minutes, coughing up some water and getting my breath back. After that day, it took me years to be able to push the mental side of breath-holding again.

I've witnessed countless beatdowns out at Shippies that have left me rattled. Watching people wipe out, wondering about the damage they have inflicted upon themselves. I couldn't put it down to one, but there's probably one from every person that's charged down there. If you wanna play, you gotta be willing to pay.

RL: What's the story behind Pedra?

MARTI PARADISIS: Pedra was like a mythical wave for many years. We are lucky to be friends with an amazing skipper/captain down here

named Dave Wyatt. He has led us on many adventures, showing what our amazing coastline may have to offer. My friend Nick "Harry" Harris started deckhanding for Dave, and they would go down off this rock to catch their cray bait. One trip, Harry came in and told me that he had seen Pedra breaking and couldn't believe how legitimate it was. I was skeptical, so I gave him my little Sony Handycam and asked him, next time he went out, to film a couple of waves. After his next trip, I watched the footage. It was only just breaking, but you could see there was bottom out there, and definitely potential for some type of right-hander. From that moment onwards, we studied the weather patterns, looking for that moment where conditions aligned. Because it is so far out to sea, we looked for light winds and a super-clean groundswell, and we realized finding the right day might take a while.

RL: How was the first mission out there?

MARTI PARADISIS: Our first mission to Pedra was in October 2008. After a year of waiting for that perfect swell, it finally came. Dave Wyatt showed us the way while Harry was deckhand and also my ski driver. Tyler and James Hollmer-Cross teamed up, along with Tom Carroll and Ross Clarke-Jones. Stu Gibson shot stills, and Andy Chisholm shot video. It was a day to remember. Conditions were perfect. A groomed groundswell with thirty- to forty-foot faces and dead glass. We surfed from sunup till the wind came in, about 2 p.m. We haven't had conditions that good since that day—almost six years ago, now.

RL: How about the highlight sessions since?

MARTI PARADISIS: The last three sessions we have had out there, the boys have truly pushed

the boundaries. Dave Wyatt skippered the vessel Velocity on each occasion. October 2012, I caught a wave that won the 2012–'13 Oakley Big Wave Awards. October 2013, Tyler caught a wave that won the 2013–'14 Oakley Big Wave Awards. And in February 2014, James Hollmer-Cross took the gnarliest beatdown I've seen out there yet. . . . Each session, Danny Griffiths goes berserko on his backhand. Plus there are the other locals that charge the spot, including Dustin Hollick, Brooke Phillips, Mikey Brennan, Shaun Wallbank, and Alex Zawadzki.

RL: It looks like such a hard-hitting, dangerous wave.

MARTI PARADISIS: Pedra is so close to being a nine-out-of-ten big-wave slab. The takeoff is a proper flat-bottom dredge, but it's so hard to pick the ones that don't shut down. Not only that, it has

this crazy backwash. It has a pretty horrific injury tally. It's only been surfed seven times and there's been three broken legs, multiple torn muscles, a number of concussions, and a broken tow board.

The power of Pedra is ridiculous; I've never experienced anything like it. The wave is traveling so quick, sometimes it's impossible to catch the wave—even being towed. You're bobbing in the middle of the ocean with seals and seabirds everywhere and these two big rocks protruding from the water. You try not to think of all the shark sightings the fisherman have told you about and concentrate at the task on hand. Doesn't get any wilder than that! But each session I have out there, as I look around, I really appreciate how beautiful the place really is and find myself having a little time-out to just look around and take it all in.

AFTERWORD
BY GREG LONG

OVER THE COURSE of the last ten years, waves never thought surfable have been tackled, world record wave heights have been broken, drops and barrels once believed impossible have been made, and the legends and lore of big-wave surfing have grown with every new swell.

The big-wave bar has been raised so high, it has left onlookers and big-wave surfers alike to question, "What's next?" Where does the sport go from here? How can it get any bigger or heavier than it already is?

Within the heart of most big-wave riders, there exists a desire to seek the greatest physical and mental potential as a human being and surfer. From this desire, and from the personal quest for greatness and profound exhilaration, stems the motivation to venture into the heaviest of lineups time and again, stepping beyond comfort zones, embracing fears, pushing the level of the sport to greater heights. It is this motivation that will continue to fuel the fire and progress of our singular pursuit.

In big-wave surfing, we are only limited by our imaginations, personal desire, and the forces of nature that provide an arena in which we test the limits of what can be achieved with each successive swell.

For more than a decade, during nearly every significant swell that Mother Nature has thrown our way, there were those who believed they could ride the impossible, and they did. I am certain this will continue to be the standard for years to come. I can't say exactly what's next. I just know that at the end of each year's big-surf cycle, we will likely be asking ourselves yet again, "What's next?"

OPPOSITE: Greg Long

PAGES 230-231: Mark Healey, caught inside at Cloudbreak.

ACKNOWLEDGMENTS

Insight Editions would like to thank all of the individuals who have made this book possible. A huge thanks to all of the photographers whose work colors these pages—your documentation of big-wave surfing inspires awe and is instrumental in individuals pushing the limits and taking the pursuit to ever-higher levels. Much gratitude to all the surfers who lent their stories and insights to this project, you were integral to telling the tale of modern big-wave surfing. Thanks to Tom Carroll for his contribution and veteran perspective, as well as Greg Long for his look at the future of the sport. And a very special thanks to Rusty Long for his great storytelling and invaluable hand in bringing this incredible collection together.

PHOTO CREDITS

DOUG ACTON: Page 27

BRUNO ALEIXO: Page 185 (bottom)

ALEJANDRO BERGER: Page 71 (top)

BRENT BIELMANN: Page 124

ROBERT BROWN: Pages 18–19, 22–23, 24, 26 (bottom), 34–35, 38, 39, 42 (bottom), 50, 52–53, 54–55, 56–57, 59, 73, 74 (top), 112 (top), and 113

ERIC CHAUCHÉ: Pages 158–159, 162, 163, 164, 165 (bottom and second from top), and 166

RAY COLLINS: Pages 211 and 212–213

ALFREDO ESCOBAR: Pages 153, 154, 155 (top), and 156–157

JEFF FLINDT: Pages 74 (bottom) and 182 (top)

HANK FOTO: Pages 102 and 105 (bottom)

ANTHONY FOX: Pages 188 and 189

STU GIBSON: Back cover and pages 196–197, 214–215, 216–217, 218–219, 220–221, 222–223, 224–225, and 226–227

TODD GLASER: Pages 13, 14, 25, 32, 40, 64–65, 66, 67 (top), 78 (bottom), 83, 89, 90–91, 93, 96, 100, 133, 134–135, 136–137 (top), 138–139, 140–141, 148, 149 (bottom), and 229

TED GRAMBEAU: Pages 150–151

ALAN VAN GYSEN: Pages 190 (top), 192, 193 (top), 193 (bottom), and 194

RICHARD HALLMAN: Page 47 (top)

YASHA HETZEL: Pages 152 (top) and 155 (bottom)

ROB KEITH: Pages 68–69

JEREMIAH KLEIN: Page 103

RUSTY LONG: Pages 22 (top left), 36, 41, 42 (top), 51 (top), 58, 62–63, 71 (bottom), 72, 75 (bottom right), 88 (top), 132, 136 (bottom), 137 (bottom left), 152 (bottom), 173, 177, 178–179, 190 (bottom), and 195

AL MACKINNON: Pages 160–161

TÓ MANÉ: Pages 180 (top), 183, 184, and 186–187

MATT MARINO: Pages 44–45, 47 (second from top), and 48–49

BRAD MASTERS: Pages 94–95

EDWIN MORALES: Pages 78 (top), 79, 80–81, 82, and 86–87

RYAN MOSS: Page 67 (bottom)

JASON MURRAY: Pages 21 (top), 29, 60–61, 75 (top), 77, 112 (bottom), and 191

MICHAEL NEAL: Pages 111 (top), 116–117, and 126 (top)

A.J. NESTE: Pages 4 and 75 (bottom left)

CLIFF NIES: Pages 84–85

ZAK NOYLE: Pages 2–3, 97, 98–99, 101, 106–107, 108–109, 126 (bottom), and 127

RUSSELL ORD: Pages 6–7, 208–209, and 210

SHAWN PARKIN: Pages 43 and 46

FRED POMPERMAYER: Book case and pages 8–9, 16–17, 21 (bottom), 26 (top and middle), 28 (bottom), 30, 31, 37, 110, 114–115, 118–119, 121, 122–123, 125, 128–129, 137 (bottom right), 143, 144–145, 146–147, 149 (top), and 185 (top)

LAURENT PUJOL: Pages 1, 165 (top), 168–169, 174 (top), and 181

FRANK QUIRARTE: Front cover and page 70

DANIEL RUSSO: Page 104

EPES SARGENT: Pages 10–11

TOM SERVAIS: Pages 230–231

JAMIE SCOTT: Pages 198–199, 200–201, 202–203, 205, and 206–207

MICKEY SMITH: Pages 15, 170–171, 172, 175, and 176

PAT STACY: Pages 130–131 and 142 (top)

PATRICK TREFZ: Pages 20 and 92

INSIGHT
EDITIONS

PO Box 3088
San Rafael, CA 94912
www.insighteditions.com

Find us on Facebook: www.facebook.com/InsightEditions
Follow us on Twitter: @insighteditions

Text copyright © 2015 Rusty Long
Foreword copyright © 2015 Tom Carroll
Afterword copyright © 2015 Greg Long
All photographs copyright © 2015 by their respective photographers cited in the photo credits

All rights reserved.

Published by Insight Editions, San Rafael, California, in 2015. No part of this book may be reproduced in any form without written permission from the publisher.

Library of Congress Cataloging-in-Publication Data available.

ISBN: 978-1-60887-409-5

PUBLISHER: Raoul Goff
CO-PUBLISHER: Michael Madden
ACQUISITIONS MANAGER: Robbie Schmidt
ART DIRECTOR: Chrissy Kwasnik
DESIGNERS: Kris Branco and Jon Glick
EXECUTIVE EDITOR: Vanessa Lopez
PROJECT EDITOR: Dustin Jones
PRODUCTION EDITOR: Rachel Anderson
PRODUCTION MANAGER: Jane Chinn

ROOTS of PEACE   REPLANTED PAPER

Insight Editions, in association with Roots of Peace, will plant two trees for each tree used in the manufacturing of this book. Roots of Peace is an internationally renowned humanitarian organization dedicated to eradicating land mines worldwide and converting war-torn lands into productive farms and wildlife habitats. Roots of Peace will plant two million fruit and nut trees in Afghanistan and provide farmers there with the skills and support necessary for sustainable land use.

Manufactured in China by Insight Editions

10 9 8 7 6 5 4 3 2 1